DESCARTES' *MEDITATIONS*

Nat Mansfield

07957126307.

Continuum Reader's Guides

Continuum's *Reader's Guides* are clear, concise and accessible introductions to classic works of philosophy. Each book explores the major themes, historical and philosophical context, and key passages of a major philosophical text, guiding the reader towards a thorough understanding of often demanding material. Ideal for undergraduate students, the guides provide an essential resource for anyone who needs to get to grips with a philosophical text.

Reader's Guides available from Continuum:

Aristotle's Nicomachean Ethics – Christopher Warne

Berkeley's Three Dialogues – Aaron Garrett

Deleuze and Guattari's Capitalism and Schizophrenia – Ian Buchanan

Hegel's Philosophy of Right – David Rose

Heidegger's Being and Time – William Blattner

Hobbes's Leviathan – Laurie M. Johnson Bagby

Hume's Enquiry Concerning Human Understanding – Alan Bailey and Dan O'Brien

Hume's Dialogues Concerning Natural Religion – Andrew Pyle

Kant's Critique of Pure Reason – James Luchte

Kant's Groundwork for the Metaphysics of Morals – Paul Guyer

Locke's Essay Concerning Human Understanding – William Uzgalis

Locke's Second Treatise of Government – Paul Kelly

Mill's On Liberty – Geoffrey Scarre

Mill's Utilitarianism – Henry West

Nietzsche's On the Genealogy of Morals – Daniel Conway

Plato's Republic – Luke Purshouse

Spinoza's Ethics – Thomas J. Cook

Wittgenstein's Philosophical Investigations – Eric James

Wittgenstein's Tractatus Logico-Philosophicus – Roger M. White

DESCARTES' *MEDITATIONS*
A Reader's Guide

RICHARD FRANCKS

continuum

Continuum International Publishing Group
The Tower Building   80 Maiden Lane
11 York Road   Suite 704
London SE1 7NX   New York, NY 10038

www.continuumbooks.com

British Library Cataloguing-in-Publication Data
A catalogue record for this book is available from the British Library.

ISBN-10: HB: 0-8264-9283-5
PB: 0-8264-9284-3
ISBN-13: HB: 978-0-8264-9283-8
PB: 978-0-8264-9284-5

Library of Congress Cataloguing-in-Publication Data
Francks, Richard.
Descartes' *Meditations* : A Reader's Guide/Richard Francks.
p. cm.
Includes bibliographical references (p.).
ISBN 978-0-8264-9283-8 — ISBN 978-0-8264-9284-5
1. Descartes, René, 1596–1650. Meditationes de prima philosophia.
2. First philosophy. I. Title.

B1854.F68 2008
194--dc22

2007050014

Typeset by Newgen Imaging Systems, Pvt Ltd, Chennai, India
Printed and bound in Great Britain by MPG Books Ltd,
Bodmin, Cornwall

CONTENTS

How to Read This Book   vii
References, Quotations and Abbreviations   viii

1. The *Meditations* in Context   1
2. Overview of Themes: The Problem of Objectivity   5
3. Reading the Text   9
   Part I: The Doubt   9
   Part II: The Self   45
   Part III: God   89
   Part IV: The Possibility of Knowledge   129
   Part V: The Nature of Matter and the Certainty of God   146
   Part VI: The Existence of Matter   159
4. Reception and Influence of the *Meditations*   172
5. Further Reading   179

Notes   183
Index   192

HOW TO READ THIS BOOK

The best way to read this book is as follows.

- Read (or re-read) the first section of the *Meditations*.
  - The 'sections' are my invention, and won't be marked in your text. Look at the Section heading to see where it is.
- *Write down* what it says, and then write down *what you think* about what it says.
- Read my Overview of the section, see how it compares with yours, and note the differences.
- Read the Commentary on the section, and write down what it says and what you think of it.
- Repeat for the remaining sections of Meditation 1.
- Read the Discussion sections, one at a time, and write down what they say, and what you think about them. Alternatively, follow the Links at the ends of sections and read the Discussions if and when they catch your interest, or relate to what you're thinking about.
- Repeat for the rest of the book.
- *But of course*, most people don't do most things the best way – they read the bits they're interested in, bits they're told to read or bits they think might help with whatever they're working on. So I've tried to organize the book as a series of bite-sized pieces with links and cross-references which should enable you to get from it whatever you need.
- *Overviews* give a fairly crude paraphrase of what I think are the main points Descartes is making in each section.
- *Commentaries* set out what you need to think about to understand each section – how it relates to earlier and later parts, what it means, what questions it raises for us.
- *Discussions* are a rag-bag of follow-up materials, usually either explaining some of the background, developing some of the ideas raised or a combination of the two.

REFERENCES, QUOTATIONS AND ABBREVIATIONS

References to Descartes' texts use the volume and page numbers of the Adam and Tannery edition, (see Chapter 5), which should enable you to locate them in most modern English versions. For example, 'IXb. 46' means page 46 of volume 9b. Where no volume number is given, the reference is to volume VII. In the case of the *Principles*, which is divided into short sections, I have given only the part and section numbers.

Quotations are taken from the Cottingham, Stoothoff and Murdoch translation (where the Adam and Tannery page numbers are the ones given in the margin).

References in round brackets – such as (54) – give the source for a quote, or the evidence for an assertion. Those in curly brackets – {OR5, 336} – give cross-references to where the same or similar points are made. Those in square brackets – [3.3.2] – refer to other parts of this book where the topic is covered.

For Abbreviations, see Chapter 5.

CHAPTER 1

THE *MEDITATIONS* IN CONTEXT

1. 1596–1650

René Descartes was born in 1596, and died in 1650.

What does that mean?

It means he was born in the decade when in France the Wars of Religion ended and Henry IV ('of Navarre') came to the throne; when Elizabeth I reached 40 years on the throne of England; when Walter Raleigh sailed 300 miles up the Orinoco, and the English Army abandoned the bow as a weapon of war. He was born when Shakespeare was writing plays, Byrd and Dowland were writing music, and Caravaggio, El Greco and Tintoretto were all painting.

His lifetime saw the Thirty Years War; the execution of Charles I in England and the coronation of Louis XIV in France; the arrival in America of the first English settlers and the first black servants; and in Europe of China tea, and coffee. Of more direct relevance, it also saw Harvey's treatise on the Circulation of the Blood, the cosmology of Tycho Brahe and Kepler, the physics and astronomy of Galileo and the increasing acceptance among learned people (despite its prohibition by the Pope) of a 'Copernican' view of the Earth as not being the fixed centre of a closed Cosmos, but a planet orbiting the Sun in a limitless universe.

2. LIFE OF DESCARTES

Descartes was the third surviving child of a relatively rich family (until he sold the land and title, he was the Seigneur du Perron) in Touraine, Western France. His mother died when he was only 1-year-old, and he was brought up by his grandmother. He seems to have been of a sickly, nervous disposition, and to have gone through periods of intense, feverish study and at least one nervous breakdown. For some years he considered a legal or administrative career, but in the end decided to live on his relatively modest inheritance, and to devote himself to his studies. The only career he ever had was as a military engineer in different armies during the Thirty Years War, which enabled him to travel around Europe and meet various learned persons. Although he was present at the siege of La Rochelle in 1628, he seems to have avoided any direct involvement in fighting. Thereafter he settled in the newly independent Dutch Republic, where he lived for 20 years (with great secrecy as to his precise whereabouts, and frequent changes of address), until he accepted an invitation to be a kind of personal tutor to Queen Christina of Sweden. He died of pneumonia within 6 months of arriving in Stockholm. He never married, and his relationships with men were often problematic, characterized by intense affections and bitter recriminations. His only child, a daughter (her mother was a servant in a house in Amsterdam where he stayed) died when she was 5 years old.

3. HIS WORK, HIS FRIENDS AND HIS ENEMIES

1. His Life's Work

For all his fame as a philosopher, Descartes himself was in our terms primarily a mathematician and physicist. He wrote books and treatises on, among other things, what we would call Psychology, Geometry, Mechanics, Physics, Anatomy, Music, Cosmology, Ethics, Meteorology and Optics. As a mathematician he was the founder of Analytical Geometry, and his Physics was the basis of all work in the area at least until Newton. For our purposes, though, what is most important about what he wrote is not what we would now call his scientific work, but the efforts he made to ground, legitimize, popularize and defend it. Those efforts produced what we call his philosophical works, and of those the most famous is the *Meditations*.

Although he may have been a rather shy and nervous character, he was a man of great intellectual arrogance. Like many wealthy young laymen of the time he was convinced that the orthodox Christianized Aristotelian science of his day was completely mistaken [3.1.11], and by his mid-thirties he had come to the conclusion that he had discovered the whole truth about how the world really works, and that he alone could provide the one true explanation for the whole physical world. Unfortunately before he could finish writing up his discoveries, news arrived that Galileo had been condemned by the Church for defending the idea of a moving Earth, and since that idea was an essential part of his own new theory of life, the universe and everything,[1] he came to the conclusion that the world was not yet ready for what he had to tell us, and gave up in despair.

But although he was terrified of controversy, he was perhaps even more frightened of obscurity; so, quite soon he started to think about other ways of getting his message across. He was sure that his view of the nature of the world was correct, and also sure that his conclusions were compatible with, and indeed were identical with, the teachings of the Church. The problem, he decided, was that other people couldn't see it because they were blinded by their presuppositions in other areas. That meant that in order to convince them of his physical theory he would need to start further back, and to present his explanation of the relation of God to the world, the nature of human beings and their place in the universe, and a detailed account of the possibility, nature and scope of human knowledge. So that's what he did. And by doing so, he became what we now call a philosopher.

2. The 'New Philosophy' and Its Opponents

In his Mathematics and Physics, Descartes was one of the most significant contributors to the mass of scientific, social, political, psychological and philosophical changes that historians used to refer to as the 'Scientific Revolution'. And the philosophy he developed in support of that work makes him that Revolution's first and greatest theoretician. At the heart of those changes, perfectly encapsulated in the case for the moving Earth, was a revival of the Platonic idea that the knowledge of nature requires more than a thorough cataloguing of the various systems and processes of the visible world. In order to *understand* what we see around us we need in addition to develop a knowledge of the *in*visible things that underpin it – the microscopic and submicroscopic particles, the inconceivably small and the inconceivably distant, the invisible forces and the timeless laws that govern them all.

That idea, which was central to the Magical tradition in science and strongly linked to mysticism in religion, was prominent in the thought of educated middle-class laymen of the 'New Philosophy' like Kepler and Galileo, whose work Descartes enthusiastically supported; and it was bitterly opposed by the conservative, rational, Aristotelian tradition that dominated the Church, and therefore the universities ('The Schools'), at the time. Descartes fought all his life against those conservative, 'Scholastic' elements, (even though because of the political power they derived from the authority of the Church, it was a battle he fought with one hand behind his metaphorical back), and that is the first set of enemies we need to keep in mind in relation to his writings, and to the *Meditations* in particular [3.1.1]. And as with all revolutionaries, the second set of enemies he is fighting against is another faction on his own side. Among those who like Descartes and his friends were calling for the overthrow of traditional learning were those who thought not that we should go about trying to understand the world differently, but that we should give up the attempt altogether. The collapse of the old certainties led a lot of people to think that objective knowledge is unattainable, and that Scepticism rules [3.1.7].

3. Descartes and Us

Descartes' basic philosophical task, then, is to present an account of human beings, God and the world which will show that genuine, objective knowledge *is* possible if we go about it in the right way, that is, if we follow what we would call the path of science. That is the view which won out in the battle for hearts and minds in the seventeenth century. And it is the view which more than any other defines the Modern era, a view which underlies most of the traditions, institutions, languages, attitudes and habits of mind in which we live our lives [4.1]. The *Meditations* is Descartes' attempt to prove the truth of that view. If we don't find that proof convincing, we need to ask ourselves whether his view can still be sustained [Chapter 2; 3.6.5].

OVERVIEW OF THEMES: THE PROBLEM OF OBJECTIVITY

The *Meditations* is a book about Objectivity. It is about the questions whether, when, how and why we can escape from the limitations necessarily imposed on us by factors like our humanity, our individual place in the world, our personality, our upbringing and our education so as to look at the world objectively, and see things as they really are in themselves.

Those questions, which I will throw together under the title The Problem of Objectivity, seem to me to be the most pressing philosophical problems of our age. It is a common thought that the world now is much smaller than it used to be. And a consequence of that fact is that we are forced in a way that our ancestors never were to deal with the question of the Other: of how to cope with people who are different from us in ways we hadn't expected, haven't allowed for and often cannot even begin to understand.

Consider some examples, situations which are familiar to most of us.

- When you find yourself in a foreign culture, and it suddenly dawns on you that these people really are *different*. It's not just that they speak differently and wear different clothes, but they *think* differently, too. They don't believe what you believe; and that doesn't just mean that they think something is true when you think it's false, but rather that their whole understanding of things is skewed, different, out of line with yours, so that what looks at first like the same question gets a different answer. They don't even seem to *want* what you want, and it starts to feel as if they belong not just to a different race, but to a different *species*.
- When you see on your TV a report of something you find just unspeakably dreadful. You'll have to choose your own

example here – it may be child abusers, genocidal tribes, female circumcisers, rapists of old women, torturers, burka-wearers, Christians, Morris-dancers, or whatever – and you feel just baffled at the thought that there exist people who could do such things. And they seem to do them, not in desperation or when threatened or when drunk, but knowingly, thoughtfully, as a normal, sometimes even a privileged or important, part of what seem like otherwise normal human lives.

- Most obviously, there is the startling discovery that large numbers of otherwise perfectly normal-seeming people have a deep-seated and well thought-out desire to kill or maim you, even though they have never met you and don't even know your name. In spite of not knowing who you are, they want nothing more in life than to destroy you – innocent/clever/bumbling/confused you – and would happily give up their own lives for the chance to do it.

Cases like this, as soon as you start to think about them, inevitably lead us into the Problem of Objectivity. Do such instances show that people are necessarily trapped in their own little bubbles of understanding, each of us with our own separate realities which make perfectly good sense from the inside, but which are quite impenetrable to the outsider? Or should we say that the simple fact that we all inhabit a single world means there must be at least a *possibility* of agreement: there are some facts which *everyone* must acknowledge, which must be agreed from *any* point of view and which therefore prove the possibility of non-relative, non-partisan *objective* knowledge? Even where we can't establish unshakeable facts, can we at least say that in any given situation there are certain *ways of thinking* that everyone can see are better than others? Is there such a thing as an *objective* (rational? logical? scientific?) approach to a question which can be guaranteed to produce results, to lead us towards the truth and which is accessible to anyone?

Since the eighteenth century it has been very widely believed that natural science provides the model of objective thought, and of objective knowledge. Science discovers facts, it tells us how the world is and how the world works, and those things are true *objectively*, quite irrespective of who anyone is or what anyone thinks – you only have to look at the practical results of science to see that. Scientific thinking is therefore *objective* thinking, which anyone is capable of, and which tells us how things really are. More recently, though, that 'Enlightenment' view has been out of fashion. Arguments over subjects such as genetically modified crops and alternative medicine have seen many people saying that scientific thinking is limited at best; it is not an objective path to The Truth, but just one voice among many, one particular point of view on the question, to be set against those of various competing religions, creeds, attitudes or lifestyles. Others have gone further, and suggested that even in its own field, science doesn't give us an objective view of the world. Scientific theories themselves are perhaps true only relatively: they work within a particular context of thought, with their own rules and their own sets of 'facts'; they belong to a particular way of thinking that holds for a time, and then is abandoned. Scientific 'truth', therefore, is really only a kind of fashion, or tradition, and when two scientific cultures clash – such as our view of an expanding universe as opposed to the medieval picture of a closed Cosmos – it makes no sense to say that one side is objectively right and the other is objectively wrong because each is right in its own terms, in relation to its own criteria and by its own standards.[1]

Is objectivity ever possible? Is it possible to escape from your own point of view and see things as they are in themselves? If so, when, how and why? And what is the objective truth about the world that the objective view reveals?

Descartes wrote the *Meditations* to answer those questions. He lived at a time when the medieval world was collapsing, and there were massive disagreements not only about the most basic facts of nature – is the Earth the fixed centre of the universe or a planet orbiting the Sun? – but also about the methods appropriate to answering such questions, the kind of people able to answer them and the possibility of ever coming to a decision. The *Meditations* is his attempt to take advantage of the widespread doubt and uncertainty of the new intellectual public to convince them that *his* answers are the ones they should accept. And in order to persuade them of that he tackles the Problem of Objectivity. He claims that

- There are some truths that no-one can deny.
- Those truths enable us to construct a genuine, objective knowledge of nature.

- Even in questions which we can't definitely answer, there are objective, non-relative, conclusions to be drawn.

And what is important about the *Meditations* is that Descartes doesn't merely *say* these things, but claims to *prove* them. The book is a single, sustained chain of reasoning, which anyone can follow, and which he says will lead you necessarily to accept his conclusions. *My* job in what follows is simply to make that train of thought clear to a modern reader, explain some of the background which helps to understand it, and start some trains of thought about the questions it raises for us. *Your* job as you work through the argument of the *Meditations* is then to decide whether you accept Descartes' conclusions, and if not, why not.

The chances are that you will think that the argument breaks down in certain crucial areas. In particular, his defence of *Objectivity* depends crucially on his views about *God*, and about *the Human Mind*, both of which many people are inclined to reject. And these three topics, which are the three Themes of this book, set up what I think is the *Big Question of the Meditations*.

- If we don't share Descartes' conception of human beings and of their relation to the world, can we accept his defence of Objectivity?
- If not, can we find some *other* way of defending the belief in the possibility of Objective Knowledge?
- If not, should we give it up altogether?[2]

CHAPTER 3

READING THE TEXT

PART I: THE DOUBT

3.1.1 MEDITATION 1, SECTION 1. (17–18)

CLEARING OUT THE RUBBISH
Overview
My head is full of beliefs that I've picked up over the course of my life. I know that at least some of them are false. If I'm ever going to establish a secure understanding of things, I need to sweep away all this clutter and start again from scratch. So I'll go on a retreat. I'll shut myself away from the world, and try to clear my head of all my accumulated beliefs.

Commentary
Philosophy through fiction: Descartes vs. The Thinker
At the start of the story, then, Descartes says he's confused, he doesn't know what to believe. He needs to take time out from his life to clear his mind if he's ever going to get beyond the unsystematic jumble of ideas that he's grown up with.

Now, the first thing to realize about that, and about the book as a whole, is that it's a big lie – it's a fiction. Descartes at the time of writing the *Meditations* (1638–40) is in *no doubt at all* as to what he should believe: he has a carefully worked-out set of opinions about the world and our knowledge of it which he thinks is true, provable, and will stand for ever without substantial modification [3.4.5]. And neither is this tale of the tortured quest for knowledge a re-creation of an earlier stage of his life: although there was obviously a time when he hadn't discovered his wonderful new system, there is no evidence to think that at any point he went through the kind of intense and dramatic process of systematic reflection he describes here. So why does he say he did?

The *Meditations* is a work of literature, a work of fiction, designed to convince *you*, the intelligent reader, of the truth of Descartes' system.[1] He tells this story of an imaginary journey of reflection and analysis not because it is something he has gone through himself, but because he wants *you* to carry out the kind of intellectual overhaul he describes. He thinks by introducing his system in that way he can make it more readable, and can draw you into his way of thinking more effectively than if he had simply laid out his position in text-book fashion (as he did a few years later in the *Principles*).

And there is a second aspect of this deception on Descartes' part. If he is perhaps fooling us, his readers, by pretending for literary effect to have travelled this road before us, he is certainly misrepresenting his position in a far more serious way with respect to the religious and intellectual authorities of his time.

Descartes thinks those authorities are mistaken. He thinks the whole intellectual tradition they represent is nothing more than ignorance dressed up in fancy intellectual clothes and supported by bigotry and superstition. He wants to see them swept away and replaced as the founts of knowledge by his own intellectual heroes, men like Kepler,[2] Galileo[3] and – most especially – himself. But the existing intellectual authorities have real political power, and to oppose them would be extremely dangerous; so after the condemnation of Galileo by the Inquisition in 1633, Descartes abandons the direct presentation of his views, and works out more subtle ways of getting his message across [Chapter 1]. The *Meditations* is a brilliant device when seen in that light. It is presented as the diary of a retreat – a common religious format of the time. It is dedicated to the very authorities he is seeking to subvert, the Faculty of Theology at Paris.[4] And it advertises itself in its subtitle as proving the existence of God and the immortality of the soul. In reality, though, while presented in a form of which the authorities could not disapprove, it is an appeal over their heads to us, the reading public. Through the device of the troubled soul in search of knowledge, it asks you to set aside everything you have been taught and everything you have accepted on authority, and to use your native intelligence to decide for yourself what you should believe. By following the steps of Descartes' realistic but purely fictional journey you will be led to a realization that the way to knowledge is not through authority, not through tradition, not through common sense, but through the kind of rational interrogation of the world that we now think of as natural science.

As you work through the *Meditations* you need to bear in mind its fictional character if you are to understand its true purpose, and to appreciate its design. And that means keeping in mind the distinction between two very different people. On the one side we have the orthodox, hesitant, questioning 'I' figure of the book, shutting herself away from the world to sort her head out; and on the other side we have Descartes, the author, to whom none of those words can really be applied. For the purposes of this book I shall refer to those two figures as (in reverse order) Descartes, and The Thinker. And I shall talk of The Thinker as female to help keep the distinction clear.

3.1.2 MEDITATION 1, SECTION 2. (18)

THE METHOD OF DOUBT

Overview

In order to set aside my pre-existing beliefs, I don't actually have to show they're all false. If I can find some reason, however far-fetched, for thinking that one of my beliefs could be false, then I shall reject it and treat it as if it is false. Of course, it would be impossible to consider every belief I possess individually; what I'll do is look at the basic principles upon which my beliefs depend – that is, look in turn at each different type of belief I have – and see if I can find any reason to doubt beliefs of that kind.

Commentary

1. The doubt

The series of doubts that is raised in the next four pages is perhaps the most effective and best-remembered part of this or any other classic Philosophy text. A lot has been written about it, and we'll consider it in more detail later; but in order just to make sense of the text we have before us, we need to get clear about *why* the whole story begins with the process of doubting.

And in asking why the book starts with doubting, we need to bear in mind the distinction between Descartes and The Thinker [3.1.1], and ask *two* questions: What reasons does *The Thinker* give us for going through this process of doubting everything? And why does *Descartes, the author*, choose to start the book by getting us, his readers, to work through that process of doubt?

The Thinker's reasons are quite explicit, but easily misunderstood. She's aware that, like most of us, she's picked up her view of the world by a fairly haphazard process from the people around her. She's aware that much of what she believes must be false, and she lives at a time when knowledge is increasingly contested – the Church is divided, the universities are in decline, old knowledge has been rediscovered and new knowledge is being proposed. As a result, she doesn't know what or whom to believe. So the first thing she does when she starts her retreat is to try to find something – *anything* – that she can regard as certain, in the hope that she will be able to use that certain knowledge to build a more systematic and trustworthy body of knowledge – to 'start again right from the foundations' (17). And how is she going to do that? Simple: by trying to doubt everything she possibly *can* doubt, in the hope of finding something she *can't*. She will work through the different kinds of belief she possesses, and see whether she can find any reason, however improbable, why beliefs of that kind *could*, just possibly, be false. And if she can find any such grounds, she will hold off from *all* beliefs of that kind: she will suspend judgement on them until such time as she can find some way of deciding whether or not to accept them (18).

Descartes' reasons for putting us through this process, on the other hand, are tied up with his attitudes to knowledge, ancient and modern. His own theories and those of his fellow modernizers, he thinks, are based on reason and evidence, and he is confident that any reasonably intelligent person – such as you, his reader – who considers them honestly will be forced to accept them. His opponents' views, on the other hand, he thinks are nothing more than ignorant 'common sense' expressed in high-sounding but obscure language and maintained by a combination of uncritical tradition and political violence. Of course, he can't *say* that the learned fathers in the universities are talking nonsense and that we shouldn't listen to them; but he thinks he can bring us to see that for ourselves. If we go through the process of suspending our belief in anything that could possibly be false, then the views of his opponents he thinks will be chucked out pretty early on in the piece, and we will then be able to consider his own views with an open, and unprejudiced, mind – and so see that he is right.[5]

All this means that there are two things you need to bear in mind in order to understand the Doubt.

1. The process which The Thinker goes through, and which Descartes wants us to go through, is not a first-level, day-to-day doubt, but a second-level, philosophical one – not a doubt about the *facts*, but a doubt about our *standards* for ascertaining them.

    Take an example. At one point The Thinker says she can't be sure whether she is in fact sitting in a room by a fire, as she thinks she is (29). Now, at that point, would it be a good answer to her question for you to reassure her by pointing to the walls and the ceiling and the big yellow flickery thing in front of her?

    No, it wouldn't. That isn't the kind of doubt she's considering. The problem is not that she doesn't know how to find out whether what she's currently doing is sitting by the fire or driving a team of huskies across the Arctic, or whatever – she knows what tests to apply to answer that question every bit as well as you do. And neither is it that she doesn't have enough evidence to be sure of her conclusion – as she might, for example, if she had been kidnapped and drugged, and was just waking up to find herself tied to the chair with a sock over her head so that she couldn't be sure where she was. The problem she is concerned with is that although *she knows perfectly well* that the situation she is in meets all her criteria for being one in which she is sitting by a fire, she wants to know whether *those criteria* are in reality good enough for her to be confident of her answer. It's a question, not about the facts of the situation, but about her standards for ascertaining those facts. She's asking 'Just how secure are beliefs such as this one?', and 'How do they compare with other kinds of belief I have?'.

    In other words, the Doubt is an artificial one, a theoretical one – a pretend one, so to speak. Descartes is quite clear in pointing out that he isn't really in any doubt about the facts he calls into question, and that we'd be crazy if we *really* doubted them (22). The Doubt is a *philosophical* one, an exercise, which we should all go through once or twice in our lives when we are sufficiently mature and have the time and leisure to enable us to step back from the standards we have learned to apply, and to ask ourselves just how good those standards really are, and how they compare with others[6] (17).

2. At the same time, though, it is important not to forget that it is still a very *practical*, down-to-earth question that Descartes is trying to get us to answer. The fact that this is a philosophical doubt shouldn't make you think (as many people have thought) that he is concerned only with some purely abstract, arcane, theoretical question about The Foundations of Knowledge, which is of interest to professional philosophers and perhaps to a few angst-ridden teenagers, but which has no relevance to actual daily life. On the contrary, the question he is tackling was of immediate and pressing practical significance for Descartes' readers; I think it is also of immediate and pressing practical significance for us.

The practical question to which Descartes is trying to provide an answer is the very simple one of what, and whom, to believe. Should I believe the professors in the universities, inheritors of centuries of accumulated wisdom sanctified by the Church? Should I believe the men of the New Learning (the 'New Philosophy'), with their tales of a law-governed Nature and a moving Earth? Should I take up the newly fashionable Scepticism, inspired by ancient texts and new uncertainties, and accept that knowledge is beyond us [3.1.7]? Or what should I do? The purpose of the Doubt is to get us to ask what we can really know, and how we can know it; and Descartes thinks that if we ask those higher-level philosophical questions we will under his guidance come to see that Scepticism is false, and that we *can* achieve genuine, objective knowledge of the world, but only if we abandon tradition and authority and follow the methods of Men of Reason such as himself.

The *Meditations*, in other words, far from being an abstract, other-worldly philosophical treatise, is actually a deeply political piece of writing with a clear practical objective. Its importance for us comes from the fact that his belief in the possibility of objective knowledge is something we tend to take for granted. (Do you think it's just our contemporary opinion that the Earth orbits the Sun, and that the blood circulates round the body, or that it's actually, objectively *true*?) The question we have to ask, then, is what I have called the Big Question of the *Meditations* [Chapter 2]. Does Descartes succeed in showing that we are right to think we can obtain objective knowledge? If he doesn't, can we improve on his attempt? Or should we abandon the belief?

Links

• There is more on the purpose of the *Meditations* in Chapter 2 and section 3.2.4.

2. Certainty

One further point to get clear about here is the idea of Certainty.

The Thinker wants to find out which of her beliefs are true, what she can rely on. She says she is looking for knowledge 'in the sciences' (*in scientiis*/*dans les sciences*) that is 'stable and likely to last' (*firmum et mansurum*/*de ferme et de constant* – 17). 'In the sciences' here means no more than 'in some branch of systematic learning':[7] the focus of the search is not on knowledge about what's for tea or the price of sausages, but for some unchanging facts about how things are in the world, including what we would call scientific truths – facts about the structure of the universe and of the human body, for example – and also some truths of what we would call philosophy: such questions as the nature of the human mind, and the existence of God. 'Stable and lasting' knowledge doesn't mean knowledge of some particular kind or kinds: all The Thinker is looking for is knowledge that she can be sure *is* knowledge – something she can be confident of, something that isn't going to turn out to be false. As it is often said, she is looking for something that is *certain*. 'Certainty', though, is a slippery notion, and we need to be clear what we mean by it if we're going to use it.

1. Sometimes we use it in a purely psychological sense, to express how confident we feel about something: 'I'm certain he'll turn up', 'I'm absolutely certain it isn't going to rain'. But that's not what matters here. What The Thinker is looking

for is not just something she *feels confident* about, but something she is *justified* in feeling confident about – something she has good reason to believe, something she can persuade us of, something she can *prove*.

2. But secondly, we need to be clear what *level* of certainty or justification we're talking about. Consider:

    (a) It's a certain fact that there's an eel in my sock – you can see how it's wriggling about, and if you want you can pull it out and look at it. (Though it might bite you, and your hand will get all slimy.)

    (b) It's certainly true that acceleration due to gravity on earth is 32 feet per second per second: look it up in a reliable source, or, if you like, set up experiments and measure it for yourself.

    (c) It's certain that 2 and 3 make 5 – if you don't know that, you don't know what addition is.

Are those three examples all equally certain?

We'll see later that Descartes tries to show that they aren't [3.1.3–4]. For the moment, though, what we need to be clear about is how high he sets his standards for certainty here at the start of the book. To do that, all we have to do is to look again at the way The Thinker tries to find certainty, that is, at the Method of Doubt. The Method of Doubt is the way The Thinker tests her beliefs to decide which ones, if any, constitute stable and lasting knowledge, or which ones are certain. What kind of test does it use? What level of certainty does it aim for?

The answer is that The Thinker assumes that nothing can be considered certain unless it is *beyond any possible doubt*: 'completely certain and indubitable' (18). If there is *any way I can imagine* in which something could conceivably be false, then I have to reject it as being less than certain.

Compare that with other tests for certainty we sometimes use. In English Civil Law, for example, a case is considered proven if it is true on the balance of probabilities, that is, if reasonable people, having looked at all the evidence, would come to the conclusion that it is true. In Criminal Law, by contrast, the standards are higher: a case is not proven unless there is *no reasonable doubt* about the truth of the claim in question – that anyone who had seen all the evidence and who thought otherwise would not merely have a different view, but would be acting unreasonably. How does Descartes' test for certainty compare with those?

His standard is obviously a lot higher. (He says he is looking for 'greater than ordinary certainty' – OR4, 226.) No criminal would ever be found guilty if the law required that it be *inconceivable* that she didn't commit the crime. It's not *inconceivable* that there should be someone else who had the same DNA profile and the same fingerprints as I have. It doesn't happen, but it's not inconceivable. It's not inconceivable that all the eye-witnesses who saw me do it were the victims of a mad hypnotist. It's not inconceivable that the victim was killed not by me, but by a death ray fired by little green aliens whose spaceship is invisible to all human detection systems. None of those suggestions would be admissible as a defence in a court case; but all of them are reasons why Descartes' Thinker would have to reject the belief that I committed the crime as not a piece of stable and lasting knowledge.

The standard Descartes is using here, then, is very high. As high as it could be. In setting up The Thinker's quest in this way, Descartes is implicitly claiming two things:

1. That nothing is certain – or if you prefer nothing is *really* certain – unless it is *absolutely* certain, beyond all conceivable doubt; and
2. That unless we can find something which is Absolutely Certain in that sense, we have no real knowledge at all, only a mass of shifting and unreliable beliefs, none of which we can show any good reason for accepting. The only choice is between Absolute Certainty and Scepticism [3.1.7].

Are those claims true?

Links

- The possibility and desirability of Absolute Certainty are discussed in 3.1.10.
- A more advanced discussion of Scepticism and Certainty (best left until you've worked through to Meditation 4) comes in 3.4.4.
- The relation of certainty to scientific knowledge is considered in 3.4.5.

3.1.3 MEDITATION 1, SECTION 3. (18–19)

DREAM DOUBT
Overview

Now, the things I've always been most confident of are things in the world around me that I perceive through my senses – things I see, hear, feel, and so on. But I often make mistakes about things like that: I see a friend across the street, and it turns out to be a stranger; I hear demons scraping their long fingernails against my bedroom window, but it's only a tree blowing in the wind. So everything I learn through my senses is something that *could* be false, and I'll have to discount it for the purposes of my investigation (18).

> 'But hang on a minute. It's true that I make mistakes about difficult cases – people seen at a distance, strange noises heard in the night, and the like. But some sensory things I just *can't* doubt: I'd be completely mad to question really obvious things, like that I'm sitting in this room, that this is my hand in front of my face, and stuff like that.' (18–19)

No, that's a silly argument, because dream experiences are just as obvious and just as immediate as the most convincing real experiences, and yet they're all false.

> 'But I know the difference between dreaming and waking; I'm not dreaming *now*!'

Hah! And how often have I *dreamed* that I'm awake, that I've pinched myself, or whatever? In general, *any* experience I can have when I'm awake is one I *could* have when I'm asleep; so there is no way you can definitively tell one from the other. Therefore, we have to conclude that *all* my sensory experience is in principle open to doubt, and there may not be a world around me at all.

Now I'm really confused (19).

Commentary

Here for the first time The Thinker starts a little dialogue with herself, arguing the issues back and forth. It is a technique that Descartes will use often to try and draw us into his chain of thought.

Look out for it: if you don't recognize it, it is easy to miss the point of what he's saying.

The first move is the casual-looking remark that most of the time what we take as most certain is the world around us, the things we directly experience. Does that seem reasonable? Surely, The Thinker says, if everything is in question, *these* are the things I can fall back on – the ground under my feet, my hand in front of my face, the gerbil under my fingertips, or whatever it might be. In fact, though, Descartes himself thinks that those are the things we are *least* sure of. His aim is to get us to turn our attention *away* from how things look and feel to us, and to concentrate on what they are really like *in themselves*; to turn away from our subjective reactions to things and towards an *objective* understanding of them. In other words, he wants us to stop gawping at the world and taking things as we find them, the way children do, and start *thinking* about what lies behind those appearances, by the kind of rational analysis of experience that we now call scientific reasoning [3.1.11]. Here he tries to persuade you that your sensory knowledge of the world around you isn't certain; later he'll try to show that reasoning *is*.

Does he succeed in *proving* that our senses give us no certain knowledge of the world around us?

He seems to accept that the Argument from Error – the suggestion that because *some* sensory judgements are false, *all* of them are suspect – fails because there are some sensory judgements about which we *don't* make mistakes. It's true that we sometimes mistake a stranger for a friend in the distance or in the fog, for example; but when did you last think you were sitting talking to your neighbour when in fact you were speaking to a bicycle clip, or think you were sitting at home watching the TV only to realize that you were actually playing underwater tennis 20 miles away (18–19)?[8]

The Dream Argument, though, reminds us of a different kind of error, and seems to throw doubt on *all* our sensory experience, even the most obvious cases. Is it not true that any sensory experience, however obvious it is, is one you could in theory have in a dream? You could certainly *dream* you were talking to your neighbour, even if your neighbour wasn't there, or if you don't have a neighbour. And when you dreamt it, you might be every bit as confident that that is what you were doing as you would be if it really happened. In general, is it not true that

1. There is no experience you can have that you couldn't *dream* you were having
2. There is nothing in any experience you might have that tells you it is a real experience, and not just a dream[9]
3. So if every experience you ever have of it could be a dream, you don't know for certain anything at all about the world around you, or even that it actually exists at all, do you?

That is a very important move, and will determine the whole shape of the rest of the enquiry. You need to decide whether you think it is right, and be prepared to review your opinion when you see how the story develops.

Links

- The Dream Argument is discussed in 3.1.8.
- Descartes' final response to the Dream Argument comes in 3.6.4.
- The relation of the Dream Argument to Scepticism is complex. Best place to start would be 3.1.7.

3.1.4 MEDITATION 1, SECTION 4. (19–20)

SENSING VS. UNDERSTANDING
Overview

'OK, let's assume that I *am* dreaming now, and that none of this is really happening – I'm not sitting here, this isn't my hand, and so on. Perhaps I don't even *have* any hands, and I've only dreamed I have. But still, dreams only rearrange the concepts of waking experience – they persuade me I have hands when really I don't, and so on. Or they jumble together those concepts in weird ways, and I dream about talking fish and flying spiders, or whatever. So then my actual living experience is always open to doubt; but can't I still say that *the categories in terms of which I understand* that experience can't be doubted? My *experience* may be in doubt, but my *understanding* isn't!' (19–20)

'And if that doesn't work for the categories of my day-to-day understanding, surely it must be true at a deeper level. Perhaps the idea of a hand is something I *could* invent, if I had the simpler ideas of which it's made up – if not fingers and thumbs, then at least more basic concepts, like shape, size, number, time, and so on. All the concepts in terms of which I experience the world are based on fundamental ideas like those, so those things *must* be real, and beyond doubt.' (20)

'That would mean that although all our knowledge of how things are in the world – stuff like Physics, Astronomy, Medicine, and so on – is threatened by the Dream Argument, our conceptual, or *a priori* knowledge – such as arithmetic, geometry and the like – is untouched, because it's true *independently of what the world is like.*' (20)

Commentary

The only voice that speaks in this section is The Thinker's *alter ego*, as she thinks through how to respond to what I called the 'confusion' (daze/*obstupescam*/*tout étonné* – 19) which the Dream Argument has produced. Notice that she doesn't attempt to defend sensory knowledge – she accepts that the Dream Argument has completely demolished it. Instead she tries to rescue something from the ruins that she is left with when she finds that what she had taken to be her most certain knowledge has been knocked away.

What she comes up with is what I called in the Overview '*a priori* knowledge'[10] – our understanding of concepts, and of the relations between them. Perhaps I don't have any hands, and I'm just dreaming that I do. Perhaps no-one has any hands. Still, will it not be true that a hand is a certain kind of object, of a certain size and shape, that moves in certain specific ways? There may not be any such things in existence, OK; but isn't it still true that that's what a hand *is*? If so, then statements of the form 'A hand is an object of such-and-such a kind' will be true, and can be known to be true even if we're forced to give up all our sensory knowledge about what's actually going on in the world – including our knowledge of people's hands.

Does that make sense?

Perhaps it doesn't. Perhaps we should say it's crazy to talk of truths about hands, and knowledge of hands, if there are no hands in existence. What we have here is not genuine knowledge at all, you might think, but only knowledge of concepts, or of language. We know nothing at all about *hands*, only about *what we mean* when we talk about them. And knowledge of meanings, when divorced from the actual things we are talking about, is worthless at best.

Descartes sees it differently. He thinks of this kind of conceptual knowledge as what he calls 'innate', by which he means not that we are born with it, but that it is *born within us* [3.3.2]. The thought is that our knowledge of such things goes beyond anything our experience provides us with. He thinks we are born, not with the concept of a hand, and not with the more basic concepts he mentions – like space, time and number – but with the ability to create or to discover those concepts, to extract and abstract them from our experiences in a way that (he will try to persuade us later) no other creature can. And that is the basis of our reasoning, and of our knowledge of such *a priori* sciences as arithmetic and geometry.

What do you think? Is it not true that a triangle has three sides, and its interior angles add up to 180 degrees, even if there are no triangles in existence – in other words, in those circumstances could you not still say for certain that *if* something were a triangle, then it *would* have those properties? If so, then it seems that our rational, *a priori* knowledge survives even if we abandon any claim to knowledge of the world around us because even if no world existed, there would still be *something* we knew for certain to be true. In the same way, don't you know for certain that *if* you have 7 bananas and 7 more bananas *then* you are the lucky owner of 14 bananas? And that if a whale is bigger than a bicycle, and a bicycle is bigger than a duck, then a whale is bigger than a duck? And don't you know those things quite irrespective of whether you are awake or asleep, and of whether there really are any bananas, whales, ducks or bicycles anywhere in existence?

If so, then Descartes seems to be right when he claims that our rational knowledge is more certain than our sensory knowledge. *Of course* that doesn't mean that our sensory knowledge is useless, as some readers of Descartes have taken him to be saying. After all, without experience, we wouldn't be able to arrive at this kind of conceptual knowledge in the first place. How would you know what a hand is, if you hadn't seen some, and been told what they were called? More importantly, if like Descartes we want to know not just *a priori* truths, but substantive facts about how the world is, facts about the nature of the universe and our place in it, then we will have to study the world; and that means collecting observations, designing instruments and carrying out experiments to help us. But *on their own*, such observations will tell us nothing. Dogs, after all, generally have much more acute senses than people have, and in that sense make much better and more accurate observations. But they have no scientific knowledge because they aren't able to *work out the implications* of their experience so as to understand its causes [3.1.11].

That, then, is the story Descartes is trying to sell. So far he has tried to show that experience is always doubtable if we try hard enough, and that *a priori* knowledge is more certain. Is that true?

Next question: Can *a priori* knowledge be doubted *at all*?

Links

- Descartes raises doubts about *a priori* knowledge in the next section, and revives them in 3.3.1.
- His notion of 'innate' knowledge is set out more fully in 3.3.2.
- The relation between *a priori* knowledge and science crops up in various places, most fully in 3.4.5.

3.1.5 MEDITATION 1, SECTION 5. (21–2)

DOUBTING THE UNDERSTANDING: THE NATURE ARGUMENT

Overview

But here's a problem. One of the beliefs I currently have is that there is an omnipotent God who made me. If that were true, couldn't that God have given me these concepts even though there is no world they refer to, and no reality they describe?

And anyway, we've all known people who make mistakes even about things they're absolutely certain of. So why couldn't I go wrong even about *a priori* knowledge, such as mathematics?

You can't deny that suggestion by saying that God wouldn't let me be deceived: he lets me be deceived *some*times, so why not *all* the time (21)? And you can't avoid it by denying the existence of God, either: if I *wasn't* made by a good God, there's *all the more reason* to think I might make mistakes even when I'm most sure of myself. So the conclusion is that there is *absolutely nothing* among my beliefs that I can't think of some reason for doubting.

Commentary

This is a vitally important little section, but because of the way it is presented it is easy to miss what's going on. The first thought is that my rational certainties might have no relation to anything in the world ('no sky, no extended thing, no shape, no size, no place') – which is little more than the conclusion we have just arrived at with the Dream Argument. The second thought is different, and more radical: not only might my concepts have no referents, but they might also actually be *false*. Even though they seem absolutely certain, although in a sense I can't doubt them, that subjective feeling of certainty is no evidence for their being objectively *true*.[11]

This is the final stage of the Method of Doubt. Having shown that Reason is more certain than Sense, because it survives the Dream Argument, he says that even Reason itself can be called into question by this new move: couldn't I just be put together in such a way that I go wrong all the time, even about things I'm most confident of? If so, then even *a priori* knowledge turns out not to be objectively true: couldn't I be wrong even about such things as basic mathematics?

Links

• Descartes returns to this final, 'hyperbolical' doubt in 3.3.1, and finally addresses it in 3.4.1.

3.1.6 MEDITATION 1, SECTION 6. (22–3)

CONCLUSION: THE MALICIOUS DEMON
Overview

If I'm going to follow my method, then, I shall have to suspend judgement about *everything* I used to believe. Of course, I know that in reality most of it is entirely reasonable and very probably true, but for the purposes of my inquiry I shall treat it all as completely false (22).

I shall tell myself there is no God, but a supremely powerful malicious demon which spends all its time deceiving me. I shall say the world around me is all a dream conjured up by this demon, and everything I believe in is unreal, just a trick to fool me. I can't escape from these delusions to find out the truth; but I can at least fight back to the extent of suspending my judgement, so that the demon can't impose on me any more. I may have no way of knowing what's true, but at least I can hold back from believing what's false.

But that is a very painful position to be in (22–3).

Commentary
Don't be deceived by the Malicious Demon

Where does all this leave us, then? What position have we got to if the arguments of The Thinker work? The figure of the Malicious Demon (*genium malignum*/*mauvais génie*, sometimes translated as Evil Genius) is one of the best-known images in the whole of philosophy, and it is easy to come away from Meditation 1 with a vague idea that Descartes thinks we can't know anything because we might be deceived by a malicious demon. But he doesn't. Two points to grasp.

1. Look carefully at the text. What part does the Demon actually play in the argument of Meditation 1? What step of The Thinker's chain of reasoning turns on it?

    The answer is that it plays no part at all. Look at the text. All the work of undermining our knowledge is done by the Dream Argument, which knocks away the certainty of our senses, and by the Nature Argument, which says we can't be certain about reason, either. The Demon only appears here at the end, as a kind of summary of the position reached, and as a reminder to The Thinker not to slip back into her old habits of thought.[12]

    And what is the position she tries to keep in mind by pretending that a Malicious Demon is deceiving her? Just what we have seen – that *nothing* is certain, so that although on a day-to-day level we do know how to ask and answer questions, nevertheless when we think philosophically we see that there is no perfect standard against which we can measure other knowledge claims, and so there is no possibility of any principled way of reconciling all the different competing claims on our credence. Should we listen to tradition, to common sense, to the teachers in the universities, to the new men of science, to the Church, to our own hearts, to the wise woman down the road or the smelly old geezer in the street who claims to have found The Answer in his trousers? We have no way of telling. We just have to accept that there is no way of deciding.

2. The position we are left in, then, although it is noticeably different from many positions that have been given that name, can fairly be called a Sceptical conclusion [3.1.7]: we have no way of getting to the truth, nothing but a mass of conflicting opinions and prejudices; we all have our subjective convictions, but there is no possibility of objective knowledge. We have as little prospect of achieving any stable and lasting knowledge as we would if a malicious demon were deceiving us at every turn.

Is that conclusion justified?

Links

- Different forms of Scepticism are set out in 3.1.7.
- The kind of doubt often associated with the Malicious Demon is discussed in 3.1.9.

***

By the end of Meditation 1, then, The Thinker has argued her way to the following conclusions, some of which Descartes will later try and show are in fact mistaken.

1. The Dream Argument shows that your sensory knowledge is not absolutely certain.
2. It also shows that it is not absolutely certain that the material world actually exists.
3. Your sensory knowledge is less certain than your *a priori*, conceptual knowledge.
4. But the Nature Argument shows that *a priori* knowledge is not absolutely certain, either.

5. So we have no absolutely certain knowledge.
6. So we have no way of deciding between conflicting knowledge claims: there are many different ways of finding 'knowledge', but no good reason to prefer one to another. So there is no genuine, objective knowledge at all.

Do you accept these conclusions, or do you see some flaw in the train of thought which leads The Thinker to them?

3.1.7 DISCUSSION 1

SCEPTICISM: WHAT IS IT? IS IT TRUE?

The Doubt of Meditation 1 raises the big, difficult question of Scepticism, which has long been seen as central to the study of Descartes and the *Meditations*. You need to get clear on what it is, and how it relates to the text.

1. 'Sceptical' Theories in General

Scepticism has had a very bad press in Western Philosophy. An awful lot of ink has been used on the question of whether and how it can be defeated, with surprisingly little attempt to say exactly what it is, or why defeating it would be such a good thing.

The central idea is very simple: a 'Sceptical' position is any theory which holds that people don't know stuff. The most extreme form of Scepticism is the suggestion that human beings don't actually know anything at all – we think we do, but we don't. Knowledge is beyond us: all we have is a bunch of beliefs, appearances, prejudices or impressions, but no actual knowledge. Less radical versions allow that we can know *some* things, but not as much as we normally think – or as we would like to think. This could be a general claim about the weakness of our faculties, or more often a worry about a particular type or area of knowledge. So a Moral Sceptic is someone who claims we can never know right from wrong, or good from bad. (Either because there are no rights and wrongs, and so there's nothing there for us to know, or because if there are such things, we can't find them out.) A Sceptic about Other Minds suggests we can never know what goes on in other people's minds – or indeed whether *anything at all* goes on in other people's minds. A Sceptic about the

External World thinks we can know what goes on in our heads, but nothing about the world outside. And so on.

2. Scepticism before Descartes

The early, Greek Sceptics tended to see themselves not as big, bad bogeymen inventing theories to frighten people into producing refutations of their views, but as serious thinkers putting forward a reasoned position which if accepted would help people to live better, happier lives. Their basic thought was that sorrows of all kinds come in one way or another from people's convictions – that it is because of what we *believe* that we fight, because of what we *expect* that we are disappointed, because of what we *find out* that we are sad, and so on. If only we could avoid being convinced of anything, if we could suspend judgement on all questions, then we could escape the bad things in life, and live as calmer, happier people. The Sceptics therefore drew up sets of arguments designed to weaken our beliefs – reminders of how fallible we are, how many sides there are to each question, how difficult it is to be sure of anything, and so on, with the intention that they might help to liberate us from the pains that come with believing.

In Descartes' day Scepticism had something of a revival, partly due to the publication in 1569 of the rediscovered works of the early Greek sceptic Sextus Empiricus. In a world in which accepted certainties were increasingly called into question, arguments which seemed to show that knowledge is beyond us, that nothing is certain, and that it is a mistake even to hope for answers to any question came to seem attractive to many people. Philosophers like Descartes, who wanted to overturn the old knowledge, had to beware of people who accepted what they said just as further evidence to show that no-one knows anything at all {OR7, 548–9}.

3. Three Scepticisms

Descartes, then, wants to prove that Scepticism is false: that we *can* establish genuine and lasting knowledge, but only if we abandon traditional methods and follow the way of what we would now call science. To do that, he tries to use Sceptical arguments to make his point: in Meditation 1 he raises the strongest Sceptical arguments he can think of, with the aim of showing (in Meditation 2 and after) that *even with those* you can't deny that we can have genuine, objective knowledge.

Some people think the arguments of Meditation 1 are too powerful, and that he never succeeds in extricating himself (or us, if we follow him) from the position he reaches at the end of Day 1 of the Retreat. But exactly what position is that? Here are three Sceptical hypotheses we need to keep separate.

A. *Global Scepticism*

Global Scepticism is the simple claim that nobody knows anything. Pretty obviously, though, that means that nobody knows that Global Scepticism is true, which is a bit of a drawback: you can't coherently claim to know that nobody knows anything.

Couldn't it still be true, though, even though no-one could know it was? In fact, doesn't that make it more of a problem: it might be true that no-one knows anything, and we've just shown that it's impossible for anyone to find out!

I suspect myself that it makes no sense to suggest that something might be true if it *isn't even conceivable* that anyone should know it was true (Can something be true if no-one could conceivably ever be in a position to *say* it's true? What would the word 'true' mean in those circumstances?) [3.1.9]. But leaving that aside, consider this objection: if Global Scepticism is true, then no-one knows anything. But then, not only does it follow that no-one knows that Global Scepticism is true, but it also follows that no-one even knows *what it means* to say that Global Scepticism is true. Or false. Or anything else, for that matter. So if Global Scepticism is true, no-one has ever known what they meant by anything they have said, heard – or even thought. (Including, of course, anyone who had the thought that Global Scepticism is true. Or false.) So if Global Scepticism is true, it's unintelligible. And things that are unintelligible *can't* be true – or false – can they?

Descartes never even mentions this kind of nonsensical, global doubt. The nearest he comes is when The Thinker's *alter ego* says she'd be mad to doubt things like the piece of paper in her hands, and the like (18–19). Descartes *doesn't* use that possibility as a further ground for doubt (any of my beliefs could be false because my brain could have been 'damaged by the persistent vapours of melancholia' – 19) – instead The Thinker says no, it isn't crazy to doubt them because I could be dreaming. Similarly, when the Malicious Demon is brought in to summarize the complete loss of confidence at the end of Meditation 1, the suggestion is not that the Demon might be messing with my head and corrupting my thought processes, so that I can't even think coherently; only that it might intervene in such a way as to make sure that no matter how coherently and carefully I think, I might still go wrong, even about the things I am most certain of. To doubt whether you can even think coherently would involve doubting even *that* thought; and like the thought that Global Scepticism is true, that seems to me to become meaningless.[13]

B. *Generalized uncertainty*
Yet when we read Meditation 1, the position of 'inextricable darkness' that The Thinker leads us into doesn't seem to be either paradoxical or nonsensical. I think that's because it isn't a position of Global Scepticism. The Thinker is facing the possibility that *nothing* she has previously held true can withstand her doubts, that *nothing* meets her criteria for certain knowledge. If that is so, then she concludes she has no touchstone, no foundation, nothing to cling to about which she can say 'Whatever else may happen, at least I know *this* is true!' And that means that the task of the *Meditations* can't be completed: we have no way of knowing whom we should trust, what we should believe. We must just struggle along as best we can with the belief system we find ourselves in because we have no independent, objective standard by which to try and improve it.

That is indeed a kind of Sceptical position. And if you make the assumption that unless we have some way of proving our knowledge, some way to demonstrate that our way of thinking is the right one, then we have no real knowledge at all; you could even say that it amounts to saying that no-one *really* knows anything. But that is very different from the kind of Global Scepticism that we have just been discussing. In particular, it is completely unaffected by the anti-sceptical argument I gave. There is *no* obvious incoherence or paradox in asserting that although people have relatively stable belief systems and sets of belief systems, each with established criteria for deciding what is to count as true and what as false, nevertheless there is no objective, system-independent test they can apply which will enable them to say which system is the correct one. Descartes treats that, what you might call 'Relativist', position as equivalent to total Sceptical despair. Is he right?

C. 'Cartesian' Scepticism, and brains in vats

But neither of those two positions is what is usually meant by philosophers who talk of Cartesian Scepticism. What they generally have in mind is the position discussed in 3.1.9. Nowadays it is usually made in terms of the hypothesis of a person who has been killed one night while asleep, but whose brain is kept alive by artificial means (in a vat). The brain is then wired up to a machine which provides it with exactly the same kind of neural impulses as the person would have had if she had been going about her normal life. The question is: if the job were done well, would it not be for that person just as if she had woken up the next day and were living a normal life? The point of the story, of course, is that if the unfortunate victim has no way of knowing that she is in fact dead and her brain is being fed artificial experiences, then none of us has any way of knowing it hasn't happened to us, either.

Is there any way to refute Cartesian Scepticism?

Links

• 'Cartesian' Scepticism is discussed in 3.1.9.

3.1.8 DISCUSSION 2

THE DREAM ARGUMENT: WHAT, IF ANYTHING, DOES IT PROVE?

In the Commentary [3.1.3] I drew three conclusions from the Dream Argument:

1. There is no experience you can have that you couldn't *dream* you were having.
2. There is nothing in any experience you might have that tells you it is a real experience, and not just a dream.
3. Therefore, if every experience you ever have of it could be a dream, you don't know for certain anything at all about the world around you, or even that it actually exists at all.

For the inference from 1 and 2 to 3, see 3.1.9. Here I want to look more closely at conclusion 2. Is it true?

Here's an objection that might have occurred to you.

The suggestion is that you can never know that an experience you're having is a real experience and not a dream. And that applies to *all* experiences, not just when you're a bit sleepy, tired, drunk or whatever. But is that true? Try this objection.

'It's true that the experiences I have when I'm dreaming feel like the real thing, in the sense that (most of the time, at least) they are *not* accompanied by the thought that I'm having this experience in a dream. So in that sense you could say I do 'mistake' the dream for reality. But notice that the same thing never happens the other way around. I have *never* made the mistake of thinking that a real, live, wide-awake, not-drunk-or-tired-or-sleepy experience was actually a dream. And the reason for that is that the experiences are actually very different. Waking experience is clearer, more systematic and more consistent than dream 'experience'. When I have a waking experience I am simultaneously aware of things like where I am, what I'm doing and when I last slept. My waking experiences fit into patterns, related to my past experiences and my anticipations of future experiences, whereas dreams are often chaotic, or bizarre. So it's just not true that I can never tell them apart. So Descartes' argument fails.'

'The practice of some torturers confirms this thought. Imagine you were kept in a locked room, sometimes in the dark, sometimes not and sometimes with images projected on the wall. Sometimes it's silent, sometimes very noisy and sometimes you think you hear noises but you aren't sure. Your food is drugged. In those circumstances, before too long you *really would* be unsure whether the experience you were having was real, or a dream.

'In other words, if the coherent narrative of your waking experience were taken away, you would be in the position Descartes' Thinker claims to be in; but for most of us (fortunately), we aren't.'

Does that show that the Dream Argument doesn't work?

I suspect it depends in part on what you mean by an 'experience'. Another way of putting the objection would be to say that what makes my waking experience different from my dreams is not so much *the experiences themselves*, as the ways they are connected. It is the fact that my current experience of sitting here typing fits in with other experiences that I either remember or expect, the fact that I see it as fitting into the (roughly) coherent narrative of my life, that distinguishes it from a dream. You might put the point by saying that it is the *context*, not the *content*, of experience that distinguishes waking from dreaming. Yes, it's true that there is no awareness, at least no sensation, I can have when awake that I couldn't also have in a dream – but that doesn't mean there is any danger of my confusing the two contexts. There is more to experience than bare sensations – there is the simultaneous awareness of that sensation's setting.

What do you think? Is there any reason to believe, as many philosophers have, that my experience can and must be broken down into a series of individual moments, like sensations or mental images, which can occur either when I am awake or when I'm asleep? Or should we say that experience is a richer, more complex, dynamic, interrelated network of awarenesses, and that to separate one from another is necessarily to misrepresent them?[14]

Interestingly, if the objection I have presented here makes sense, then I think it shows that what Descartes says is actually right. Descartes' ultimate purpose in constructing the Dream Argument, after all, is not to show that all of life is a dream, or that we can't know the world around us, but to persuade you that your knowledge of the world depends not, as we tend to assume, on our ability to *sense*, to *feel* what is going on around us, as an animal might, but on our ability to *interpret* those experiences, and to *understand* the relations between them. That seems very close to the distinction I have been calling that between content and context; in more Cartesian language, it is the distinction between bare, unaided experience, and the *reasoned understanding* of that experience. The story of the *Meditations* in a nutshell is that after raising the Dream Doubt here at the beginning, he spends the next four Meditations explaining and validating the possibility of such reasoned understanding as a reply to it, before finally dismissing the argument in Meditation 6 in just the way I argued here.

Links

- Descartes' reply to the Dream Argument comes in 3.6.4.
- For the difference between the Dream Doubt and 'Cartesian' Scepticism, see 3.1.9.

3.1.9 DISCUSSION 3

'CARTESIAN' SCEPTICISM: DREAMS, DEMONS, VATS AND *THE MATRIX*

The doubts of Meditation 1 throw up one of the Big Questions of Philosophy, about which a lot has been said and written. Could it not be the case that everything I take to be Reality is in fact some kind of systematic illusion?

There are various ways of raising this question. Could it not be that all of what I think of as my life is just a dream from which I might one day wake up – or worse still, from which I will *never* wake up? Could it not be that a Malicious Demon is deceiving me at every turn, casting around me this web of illusions that I can never penetrate? Perhaps my brain is being kept alive in a vat of pink, gooey stuff, and all my experiences are being fed to me through wires from the computer of a mad professor? Or perhaps, as in the film *The Matrix*, what we call Reality is just a computer-generated illusion controlled by Those in Power?

First, let's get clear exactly what is being suggested. The suggestion is not that I know nothing, or that nothing is true or that there is no reality. The idea is rather that I know *only what goes on in me*, not what goes on *around* me.

- I know my own experiences, the sensations I'm having and how they relate to each other. Of course, I don't know I'm sitting typing now because I may be dead and being fed typing-type experiences by members of an obscure branch of the Civil Service. But I do know it's those experiences I'm having, and not, for example, being-eaten-by-spiders-type experiences, or lying-in-a-pool-of-baked-beans-type experiences.

- I know my memories of previous such experiences (i.e. I know what *I currently remember* myself as having felt – which may or may not be what actually happened).
- I know what I mean by my words, and what my concepts involve. So I know logic and mathematics. (Though whether such knowledge has any relation to what anyone else thinks is a different question.)

What I *don't* know is anything at all outside my own mind: I don't know *what is causing* the experiences I am having. I notice there is a frog in my gazebo, for example. Is that because (as I normally think), I am in a gazebo, with a frog? Or is it because I'm having a dream, or being operated on by a mad scientist, or a Malicious Demon or whatever?

It seems to me that this is not a doubt that Descartes considers at all. But it is an interesting and important question to which the *Meditations* gives rise. Is there any answer to it?[15]

Here's an attempt. Archibald has read Meditation 1 and is worried that all of life might be a dream. Barbarella tries to allay his fears.

    B: 'Fear not, dear Archibald. A dream is *by definition* a state distinct from waking. If all my experiences are of the same kind, then it makes no sense to say they are all *dreams*. Consider: could it make sense to say that all the currency that has ever existed has been forged? What would that mean? Forged currency is that which is distinguished from the real thing in some way – by its origin, or its composition, or the like. If all currency is of the same kind, then it isn't forged, it's just . . . well, currency. And in the same way, if all experiences are of the same kind, then they're not dreams: they're just experiences!'[16]

    A: 'No, that's cheating. What I'm worried about is not that *there is no difference* between real experience and dreaming, just that *we can never tell* the difference. Obviously they're different states; but how do I tell them apart? How do I tell the real coins from the forged ones?'

B: 'But then the same argument applies. If we can never tell the difference, then you're right: there is no such thing as knowing this experience is a real one, and that one is a dream. But that means again that all experiences are alike in this respect, so again it makes no sense to say they're all *dreams*. You can't have it both ways: if there's no difference between sleeping and waking, then I can't worry about which state I'm in; and if there *is* a difference, then I'll be able to tell them apart if I look closely enough.'

A: 'Hmmm. Perhaps I need to put the problem differently. I agree that if there is no difference between waking experience and dreams, no difference between being in the Matrix and being out of it, then there's nothing at all to be concerned about. But what if there *really is* a difference, but some or all of the experiences I call 'real' are of the dream kind? What I'm worried about is that one day I might *wake up*, and find out that I've been dreaming all these years; one day I'll slip out of the Matrix, and find myself in a harsh, ill-lit world full of men with long overcoats and poor personal hygiene.'

B: 'OK. Now I agree we have a real doubt, because we have a real contrast. There is some conceivable situation which might arise and which worries you. You're now in the same situation as someone who fears she might have a terrible disease, or that her house might cave in. Those are genuine worries. And what would you do in those situations? Well, you'd carry out all the tests you can, to see if you're right. And if all the tests came up negative, then you'd be mad to keep worrying about it, wouldn't you? Of course, it *could* still happen – it's a conceivable state of affairs, so you can't rule it out completely – but you would have no rational grounds for thinking it *was* going to happen.

'And the same is true here. If you think you might be being deceived, then check. And if all the tests you can think of say you're not, then you have no rational grounds for the belief. It remains something that *could turn out* to be true, but to believe it *is true* would be as crazy as believing with no evidence that your house is about to be struck by lightning, or that mashed potatoes can cure cancer.'

A: 'No, no, you're missing the point. You've now turned it into just a *practical* question, about whether or not I have good reason to *expect to find out* that I've been deceived all these years. And I agree that I haven't. But what I'm worried about is the kind of problem you *can't* find out about: what if I'm in a *permanent* dream, the Malicious Demon *always* gets between me and the world – the sort of problem for which by its very nature there *couldn't* be any evidence!'

B: 'Oh Archie, do keep up. Now you've gone back to the suggestion that all the currency might be forged, and no-one could ever know.

'Think of it this way. Let's say I'm the all-powerful Malicious Demon, and I want to fool you. So I destroy the world, and replace it with a mere simulation. But then I worry that one day you'll find out – the programme will go wrong, or I'll trip over the flex and pull the plug out or something. So I hit upon the idea of destroying the world, and replacing it with a *perfect* copy, that can *never* go wrong. (I'm all-powerful, after all.) So then you could *never* tell the difference, *whatever* you did. Would I then be able to sit back and gloat about how I'd fooled you?

No. The problem is that if I did that, I wouldn't be fooling you any more, because a *perfect* copy of reality isn't an illusion, or a copy, at all.'[17]

What do you think? If you have strong 'Realist' instincts, you might think Barbarella has missed the point: whether something is true or not, or real or not, is a matter of objective *fact*, quite independent of what anyone might or ever could find out. So there is always the possibility that things are not really as they appear to us. But to make sense of that contrast between how things really are and how they are *for us* requires us to be able to make sense of the idea of an objective view of things, as distinct from any view which any person might ever actually adopt. Barbarella's 'Anti-Realist' position asks what it can mean to talk in this way of an 'objective' view. Descartes' answer is that the objective view is the view from the pure understanding of God, which the immaterial minds of human beings can share.

If you don't like that answer, how will you reply to Barbarella's question?

Links

- This line of thought comes up again in 3.4.4.

3.1.10 DISCUSSION 4

ABSOLUTE CERTAINTY: CAN WE HAVE IT? DO WE NEED IT?

1. Absolute vs. Relative Certainty

The Thinker tries to find something that is true beyond any conceivable doubt, something that is Absolutely Certain [3.1.2]. Can she succeed?

For comparison, consider first the notion of safety. When I go to sleep at night, I want to be safe. So I don't lie down in the middle of the road or in a lion's cage, I didn't buy a house on an active volcano and I don't store poisonous chemicals in my bedroom. And I generally sleep easy at night. But of course, I could be safer. There could be a gas explosion. There could be a nuclear war. The funny-looking man over the road may keep scorpions, and one might have escaped and taken up residence under my duvet. Worse still, every year in this country several people are killed in accidents involving yoghurt. I have some in my house. Clearly, I am at risk.

So what follows? Has it turned out that I am not safe after all? Should I be worried?

Not really. All these examples show is that there are different levels of safety. When we ask whether we're safe, we take for granted a certain ill-defined but robust notion of the kinds of risks we are likely to face, and the level of security we aim for. When I say I sleep safe at night, I mean I am as safe as most people, and safer than many. I am not *as safe as I could possibly be* (a nuclear shelter would be too expensive, but I *could* check for scorpions). And I am certainly not *absolutely* safe – when I am tucked up in my bed I am not guaranteed immune to any *conceivable* danger. So, should I be worried?

What would it take to make me Absolutely Safe, to put me beyond any conceivable danger?

It seems to me that the idea makes no sense. If I am rich enough and anxious enough, I can protect myself from a certain level of nuclear fallout for a certain length of time. But I can't protect myself from a direct strike by a nuclear weapon. I can't save the Earth from being hit by giant asteroids, or from being demolished by Vogons. I can't prevent the Universe from imploding. And the reason I can't do those things is not just because it would be too expensive, or I don't have the scientific understanding or the technical resources to do it: as long as I am a finite object, it will *always* be conceivable that some other object should come along and do me harm, so that Absolute Safety, safety beyond any conceivable hazard, is not only hard to achieve, but it is also not even a coherent target to aim for.

In other words, the concept of safety is essentially a *relative* one. To describe something as safe is always, and necessarily, to say that it is beyond the reach of a particular (more or less roughly defined) danger or set of dangers, not to say that it is beyond any danger whatsoever.

Now, the question is: does the concept of certainty work in the same way as that of safety? Should we say that Absolute Certainty of the kind that The Thinker of the Meditations looks for is as unattainable as I have argued the concept of Absolute Safety is? Is certainty too always and necessarily a relative notion?

2. Relative Certainty and Scepticism

At the end of Meditation 1 The Thinker is confronting the possibility that there is *no* Absolute Certainty, that none of her beliefs is true beyond any conceivable doubt. She will later change her mind about that, but it's worth asking ourselves what would follow if she were right. If all certainty were relative certainty, what would that mean for knowledge in general?

The Thinker's conclusion is that if nothing is Absolutely Certain, then everything is in doubt – she has no way of deciding which of the competing claims on her credence to accept. Scepticism rules, there is no possibility of establishing stable and lasting knowledge, and we can only throw up our hands in despair [3.1.6].

Is that true?

It seems to me not to follow without some further argument. After all, if I am right that there is no such thing as absolute safety, it doesn't at all follow that we can't tell when we are relatively safe, and therefore that we can have no good reason on safety grounds for preferring Scrabble to Russian Roulette. Why then should we conclude that if we can never be absolutely certain of anything, we can never have any good reason for believing one thing rather than another, and so that I have no better reason for thinking this is a keyboard under my fingertips than for thinking it's Queen Victoria?

What reasons might someone have for saying that if there is no Absolute Certainty, there can be no knowledge? Here are some contenders. Does any of them work?

1. *By Definition.* 'Because really all knowledge – or all *real* knowledge – is Absolutely Certain. Anything that isn't Absolutely Certain just ain't knowledge, so obviously if there is no Absolute Certainty there can be no knowledge.'[18]

2. *The Regress of Justification.* 'We are only justified in believing something if we can give a reason for it. But that reason must itself be justified, so we will need another reason for believing it. That process can't just go on for ever, so in the end you have to find something that has no need of further reasons – and that can only be something Absolutely Certain.'[19]

3. *The Purity Argument.* 'Most of what we call water – the stuff in the rivers and in the taps – isn't strictly speaking water, but water combined with other stuff. (Rivers, for example, contain sludge, muck, chemicals, fish-droppings and supermarket trolleys, most rain is actually weak carbonic acid, and so on.) Real water, pure water is to be found only in laboratory samples, not in puddles. But surely it's true that if there weren't any pure water, there couldn't be any impure water either – because impure water just *is* pure water combined with other stuff. Similarly, relative certainty is just Absolute Certainty combined with other states of mind, like doubt, and ignorance. So if there were no pure, Absolute Certainty, there could be no impure, relative certainty either.'

4. *The Perfect Form Argument.* 'The concept of certainty works like that of accuracy. It makes no sense to say something is

fairly accurate unless we have an understanding of what perfect accuracy would be. We need Absolute Certainty in order to make sense of the idea of relative certainty.'

None of those arguments is explicit in Descartes, but the belief that what I am calling Absolute Certainty is both necessary and possible is built into the whole structure of the *Meditations*. I think he would have endorsed at least the last two. Does any of the arguments work? Can you think of any other reason for thinking that Absolute Certainty, unlike absolute safety, *does* make sense? If not, and there is only relative certainty, then Descartes would say there is only relative knowledge – and that relative knowledge is no knowledge at all [3.1.2].

Links

- The Thinker's claim to find Certainty is covered in 3.4.1.
- The various forms of Scepticism crop up in several places; start with 3.1.7.

3.1.11 DISCUSSION 5

REASON, SENSE AND SCIENCE

One of Descartes' main objectives in the Meditations is to get his readers to turn their attention away from their senses and to use their reason instead. As we will see later, this fits in with his Theory of *Mind* (he wants us to use our minds, not our bodies, to find out the truth [3.6.1]), his *Mechanism* (all physical processes are properly understood through mathematics, which is rational, not sensory [3.2.4]) and his *Religious* position (in understanding the world rationally rather than through our senses, we are closer to God's understanding of it [3.3.9]).

Now, we take it for granted that natural science is based on the senses, not on reason. (Surely science is based on *observation* – and observations are *sensory*, aren't they?) So when we read Descartes' insistence on the importance of reason over the senses, we tend to assume he means to deny the importance of science. Actually, though, the difference between Descartes and ourselves is not that we think science is important and he didn't (in fact, *nobody* could give more importance to natural science than Descartes did), but just that, because of the context in which he was writing, the things he needed to say in order to make that point were rather different.

I'll talk later about Descartes' own view of scientific knowledge [3.4.5]; here I want to sketch the background against which he was working, to try to show why he wrote as he did.

In Descartes' day, the acknowledged experts on life, the universe and everything were the professors in the universities, or 'Schools'. The tradition in which they mostly worked derived ultimately from Aristotle, and offered a broadly descriptive science which aimed to systematize and classify observations of nature by understanding the patterns into which they fell, and the place or function of a thing within the natural processes of which it is part – an investigation known as 'saving the appearances'.

But of course, the account I've just given means little if you haven't seen the system in action. The best way to get a grip on it is to think of what is still called Natural History: the classification of plants and animals into different genera and species on the basis of their observable characteristics. Try to imagine doing Physics that way. You would have to observe the different materials that exist in nature, and decide which ones are related and which are not, on the basis of where they are found, what they are used for, how they look and feel and taste, and how they behave. If you can make sense of that, then try the same trick with changes: imagine a system of knowledge which consists in observing the different kinds of change that occur in nature, and classifying them into different types on the basis of characteristics such as their speed, frequency and typical outcomes. If you pursued such a study, what you would end up with is a set of interrelated lists which between them covered the whole of observable nature, subdivided into classes and subclasses, overlapping and criss-crossing in various ways. And if your lists were very strongly influenced by a reverence for the learning of the past, and for the lists produced by your predecessors, then you might end up with something that resembled the work of 'Scholastic' investigators.

Descartes thought, as most people today would, that all these lists and definitions of types and families were completely worthless. And the chief reason was that he saw them as being aimed only at describing the way things are, and as making no attempt to explain *why* they are that way. He and the other revolutionaries of the time thought it was possible, if we went about it in the right way, to look *beyond* the appearances, and to discover the hidden processes which underlie and explain them – usually by considering the actions of the microscopic and submicroscopic parts of things.

The expansion of new science of the seventeenth century, in other words, was at least in part a *metaphysical* change: it was about postulating and seeking knowledge of a different level of reality, one which lies behind the observable characteristics of things, and which is often only crudely described in the language of everyday objects, and is better described in mathematical terms [3.2.4].[20]

If that sketch makes any sense at all, I hope you will see why Descartes and other revolutionary thinkers of the day saw it as their main task to tell people to stop just looking at the world, and to think about *why* things happen as they do. And that meant telling them to ignore the evident testimony of their senses – which, after all, clearly told them that the Earth stands still and the Sun moves around it (that's exactly how it *looks and feels*, after all) – and instead to use their *reason* to work out *why* things look and feel the way they do.

The distinction I am here calling that between describing and explaining runs throughout the *Meditations*, and ties in with a range of other oppositions in Descartes' thought. Track them as you work your way through the text.

Describing	vs	Explaining
Common Sense	vs	Science
The Senses	vs	The Understanding
The Eyes of the Body	vs	The Eye of the Mind
Imagination	vs	Reason
The Visible World	vs	The Invisible World
The Body	vs	The Mind
Human	vs	Divine
Subjective	vs	Objective

What I have called the Big Question of the *Meditations* [Chapter 2] is that of whether we can keep the last of those pairs if we don't want to buy into the previous two.

Links

- Descartes' account of scientific knowledge is explained in 3.4.5.
- His own mechanical model of nature is set out in 3.2.4.
- What I have called the metaphysical change from Aristotelian to Modern, Cartesian science is set out in Chapter 1, and discussed in 3.6.5.

PART II: THE SELF

3.2.1 MEDITATION 2, SECTION 1. (24–5)

THE *COGITO*
Overview

Now I'm very confused. But I shall persevere with my plan to reject as false anything that *could be* false, in order to try and find at least one thing that is certain, or at worst to find that nothing is (23–4). So I'll assume everything I see around me is an illusion; that all my memories are false; that I have no senses at all; that all the basic categories in terms of which I understand the world are imaginary. Perhaps all I can establish is that *nothing* is certain (24).

> 'Well, perhaps what I can be certain of is something beyond all those things I just listed – perhaps a God, who puts these thoughts into me.'

No – I could just make them up for myself.

> 'But then *I* exist, don't I?'

I can't – I've just assumed I have no senses, and no body.

> 'Yes. But hang on a moment: what follows from that?'

Well, surely I'm so bound up with my body and my senses that I can't exist without them. And I've persuaded myself there is nothing in existence – no world, no minds, no bodies – nothing. So surely I don't exist, either.

> 'But no. Because if I was persuaded of it, then I must have existed!'

But what if there is a Malicious Demon constantly deceiving me?

> 'In that case, I must exist, or I couldn't even be deceived! It doesn't matter how much the Malicious Demon deceives me, it can never make it the case that I'm nothing as long as I'm thinking I'm something.'

So the conclusion has to be that the proposition 'I am, I exist' must be true whenever I assert it, or think it (24–5).

Commentary

Cogito, ergo sum: *I think, therefore I am.*

This line – perhaps the most famous ever written in a philosophy book – doesn't actually appear in the *Meditations* at all.[21] But as you can see, the thought does. The basic idea is very simple, and is common to all the different formulations in the different works: if I'm mistaken, I exist; if I'm misled, I exist; if I'm doubtful, I exist. The mere fact of thinking at all, however badly, means I must exist. And in all the doubts and confusions that The Thinker has raised, this thought comes as a kind of salvation, something to cling to, the first thing she can discover: no matter how wrong I might be, no matter how confused I am, the mere fact that I'm conscious at all must mean I exist. At last I've found something of which I can be certain, something that survives all the doubts and shows that knowledge is not beyond me.

Does that strike you as persuasive? Is Descartes right that no matter how hard you try to doubt everything, you can't get away from the certainty of your own existence?

If like most people you *do* find it persuasive, can you say why? Do you have some *evidence* for it? Some *argument* to back it up? If you met someone who *wasn't* convinced, what could you say to bring out its force?

In a way, if you can answer that question, then Descartes is wrong. The role of the *Cogito* in the *Meditations* and elsewhere demands that it be entirely self-supporting – that it should be compelling *in itself*, and stand in no need of any back-up, in the sense of something else you need to consider in order for you to see that it is true. After all, at this point of The Thinker's quest, she can't rely on *anything* to support her conclusions; she is trying to find something she can't doubt, something that will serve as the foundation stone to enable her to rebuild the House of Knowledge. So if the *Cogito* doesn't work alone, it doesn't work at all. *Does* it work alone? And if so, *how* does it work? The answers are more complicated than you might have thought.

1. Is 'I exist' a Necessary Truth?

A necessary truth is something that can't be false. Something that *has* to be true, regardless. Something that would be true no matter how things were, no matter what happened. Something that is True in All Possible Worlds. Philosophers argue about what counts as a necessary truth, whether there are different kinds of them, and why they're true, but here are some uncontroversial (and trivial) examples: There is nothing that is larger than itself. A fish is a fish. Squares have four sides. Look at the first of those examples. You don't have to go out and measure things to find out whether it's true or not – you know it's true *in advance* of any test (you know it '*a priori*') because it just *has* to be true, and if your ruler told you something different, you'd throw the ruler away.

Now, if 'I exist' is a necessary truth, then it is clear why we find the *Cogito* so convincing: that would mean it *has* to be the case that I exist, it couldn't be false. And given that necessary truths are true irrespective of how things happen to be in the world, that would fit with the demand we have just articulated that the *Cogito* needs to be something that needs no evidence, something that stands alone.

The text of Meditation 2 makes it look as if this is exactly what Descartes has in mind. The Cottingham, Stoothoff and Murdoch translation says '*I am, I exist, is necessarily true* [my italics] whenever it is put forward by me or conceived in my mind' (25), and it has The Thinker wondering 'what this "I" is, that now *necessarily exists*'(25; my italics).[22]

What do you think? Is 'I exist' a necessary truth?

No, it isn't. To say that it is would be to say it was true in all circumstances, that it couldn't be false. But I don't think I'm eternal, so I think that before I was born it *was* false – I didn't exist back then. And unless I'm immortal, 'I exist' when used to talk about me will unfortunately all too soon be false again. necessary truths can't be true at some times and false at others, can't depend on how things are in the world, so 'I exist' can't be a necessary truth.

And in fact Descartes isn't suggesting that it is. His thought is not that whenever I think 'I exist' I am thinking a necessary truth, but that necessarily, whenever I think 'I exist', I am thinking a truth. See the difference? It's not that I have to exist, just that I have to exist *given that I'm thinking*. The necessity lies not in my existence (reading Descartes may be good for you, but it doesn't make you immortal), but in the *inference* from thinking to existing. ('Necessity of the Consequence', not 'Necessity of the Consequent'.)

In other words, what I'm saying is that while 'I exist' is not a necessary truth, the conditional statement '*If* I'm thinking *then* I exist' *is* a necessary truth – it's something that couldn't possibly be false, in any circumstances.

2. Is the Cogito only a Conditional Certainty?

But hang on: something's wrong here. We've now found a necessary truth, something self-standing, something we can know *a priori*, without relying on the knowledge of anything else. But it seems a lot less interesting than we thought it was. What we thought we had established was our own existence: that *I am*, I exist, I am a thing in the world, even if nothing else is. But the necessary truth we've now turned it into is only a *conditional* statement: I have established beyond doubt that I exist IF I am thinking, that thinking and existing can't be separated. But if that's all we've got, then we haven't in fact established that I actually exist at all. And anyway, didn't we manage to cast doubt on simple *a priori* knowledge with the Nature Doubt of Meditation 1 [3.1.5]?

To see that this is the wrong way to look at the *Cogito*, ask yourself this question. How does it compare with other, similar-looking 'discoveries', such as I wink, therefore I am, I stink, therefore I am, or I drink, therefore I am? Is every one of those indubitable in just the same way? After all, non-existent things don't drink, for example. So we can say for certain that if I drink, I exist, just as we can say that if I think, I exist. Does that mean Descartes could just as easily have gone for *Bibulo Ergo Sum*? (He could perhaps have been sponsored by his local vineyard.)

But no, that wouldn't work. Why not? What's the difference between I think, therefore I am, and I drink, therefore I am?

Well, simply that you can doubt whether or not you drink (or wink or stink), but you can't doubt whether or not you think. If a Malicious Demon is deceiving you at every turn, then perhaps there is no water, you have no lips, and you only *think* you've been drinking all these years. But you can't only think you're thinking; if you *think* you're thinking, then you *are*.

So the *Cogito* is turning out to be more complicated than it looks. We seem to have analysed it into a combination of two thoughts: I can't doubt that I'm thinking, and if I'm thinking, then I must exist.

3. *Is the* Cogito *an inference?*

But still we have a problem. What we've said is that the *Cogito* works because it is a combination of two thoughts, in effect an *argument*, of the form

1.   I am thinking
2.   Anything that thinks, exists, therefore
3.   I exist.

Is that what's going on? Is that why most people find it so convincing?

The problem lies in premise 2. How can Descartes' Thinker, who is so confused she no longer knows *what* she should think, take for granted this general principle about the relation between thought and existence? What happened to the Nature Argument? The *Cogito* was supposed to be the turning-point, the starting-point for all knowledge, the one thing we could be sure of if all else failed. Now it seems we can only avail ourselves of it if we have *already* managed to establish that non-existent things can't think. (I'm not suggesting it's not *true* that non-existent things can't think, only that at this stage The Thinker can't assume that it is.)

This objection was put to Descartes, and his answer is interesting. Faced with a choice between saying either that the *Cogito* is not a valid argument, or that it relies on some further knowledge, he goes for the former: he says it isn't an argument at all (OR2, 140).

He claims that the *Cogito* is not two thoughts, but one, 'a simple intuition of the mind' – something anybody can see must be true, as soon as they understand it. Elsewhere (*Principles*, 1.10) he admits that of course, you couldn't understand the *Cogito*, and know it was true, unless you already knew that non-existent things can't think – just as you couldn't understand it if you didn't know what thinking and existence are. But that doesn't mean that it's really an argument, in which you start from your pre-existing knowledge of the relation between thinking and existence, and *work out* the conclusion that you exist. On the contrary, he claims, I only know the general proposition that everything that thinks exists, because I can see that I couldn't think without existing {OR5App., IXa.205–6; OR6, 422}.

Does that seem plausible, or do you think the *Cogito* isn't self-sufficient, and so can't do its job as the stopping-point of the Doubt?

In part, what is at issue here is the difference between Logic and Psychology. Descartes is happy to say that from the point of view of Logic the *Cogito* is best represented as an argument with two distinct premises. But what does he care about Logic? What he is concerned with is the plight of the doubter, with actual people who are unsure what to believe. And he claims that, no matter what the logicians may say, it is a matter of psychological fact about all of us that no matter how hard you try, you can't doubt your own existence, because you can see that the very act of doubting is enough to prove you exist. Is he right?

Links

- A famous objection to the *Cogito* is considered in 3.2.7.
- For what exactly the *Cogito* proves, see next section.
- For the question of what we can build on it, see 3.3.1.

3.2.2 MEDITATION 2, SECTION 2. (25–9)

THE SELF

Overview

But what exactly have I proved? What is this 'I' that I have proved to exist? If this is to be my foundation, I need to be very clear what it is (25).

Well, I'm a human being. But I'm not going to go into all the theoretical stuff I've been told about biology and species and the like. Let's just look at what I *am aware of myself* as being.

Primarily I think of myself as my body. But I'm also aware that there is more to me than just the parts that make up my corpse: I am animate, or, as we say, I have a 'soul' – which means I eat, move around, perceive and think. I'm not at all clear what this soul is, but body, or matter, is easy to understand – it's just stuff: objects of different shapes and sizes which occupy space and can be moved around in all kinds of different ways. Matter can be moved, but it can't move itself, of its own accord – it's just inert three-dimensional *stuff* (25–6).

But what's left of my body if we take away everything a Malicious Demon could deceive me about? Nothing. I can doubt away every physical property I possess. What about my 'soul'? Eating, movement and sense-perception I can doubt away along with my body. The only thing I couldn't be deceived about is *thinking*: the 'I' that I have just proved to exist is whatever it is that is my conscious, thinking self – my mind, intelligence, intellect or reason (26–7).

What else can I picture myself as being? I'm not my body, and I'm not some physical thing in my body which makes it operate, because I've doubted away all matter, and I still exist.

'But if I don't know everything that makes up my body and makes it work, couldn't there be something in it that is me?'

I'll leave that aside for the moment; what I'm sure of is that *knowledge* of my self can't depend on knowledge of my body. Or on *anything* physical. So the concept of *me* is quite separate from my concept of matter; so to understand myself, I have to turn my attention away from images and imagination (27–8).

So what am I, then? Something that *thinks*. That means something that doubts, understands, affirms, denies, wants/doesn't want, has images and perceptions (28). It seems obvious that it is the same *I* who does all those things. Even images and perceptions are a kind of thinking in the following sense: I see the lamp; now, there may not be a lamp there, but still I *have the sensation* of seeing a lamp – and that too is a kind of 'thinking' (28–9).

Commentary

What exactly is it that the *Cogito* proves? If you have followed The Thinker's train of thought so far, you have arrived at the certain conclusion that you exist. But *what is it* that you thereby know exists, exactly? If *I* think through the *Cogito*, for example, do I become certain of the existence of a rather boring, nervous, ageing person who wrote a book about Descartes and was once nearly killed by a train? No, surely not. The *Cogito* can't prove that I am fat or thin, tall or short, young or old. (Perhaps I am actually young, interesting and handsome, and it's a particularly cruel Malicious Demon who makes me think otherwise.) It can't guarantee that I have a particular history – or indeed any history at all (I could have been created, with all my memories, a few moments ago). In short, it tells me only *that* I am, but gives me no indication at all as to *what* I am. All I know is that *the thing that's having these thoughts* exists – the thing that's asking itself these questions, wants to solve these problems, and is having these sensations. But apart from being a thing that thinks, I have no way of proving what that thing might actually be [3.2.7].

Later on Descartes will try and persuade us that we can know more about our selves than that [3.2.8], but at this stage he leaves it open as to what these thinking things may be like. Three things to notice for now:

1. Look at how 'the soul' here is used in a loose, everyday sense to mean whatever it is that makes the difference between a live person and a dead one. We'll see later what kind of thing he actually takes that to be [3.2.6].

2. Notice also what 'thinking' means: he uses it to cover any conscious state, including purely intellectual stuff, like doing philosophy, but also more practical things, like deciding what to have for tea, and also your consciousness of your physical states – not the actual activity of your nerves and brain itself, and the zillions of processes which go on in you as you sense and respond to the world around you, but your *consciousness* of those reactions – the *feel* of the jelly in your hand, the *sound you hear* of the fingernail scraping across the blackboard.

3. Descartes says your thinking self can't be identical with your body, because your body might not exist, and yet your thinking self certainly does. At this stage he leaves open the possibility that although my self can't be just the material thing that is my body (after all, that's the same in a dead person), it could be some physical part or process that isn't so obvious. But he does say that the fact that he knows he exists even when he doesn't know there is a material world

shows that the idea of his mind doesn't involve the idea of anything physical – a conclusion he will build on later [3.2.8].

3.2.3 MEDITATION 2, SECTION 3. (29–34)

A PIECE OF WAX
Overview

> 'But this thing I claim I know best of all, this Self, seems a strange, alien thing that I can get no clear picture of. Surely the objects around me are much better known than that!' (29–30)

Well, let's see. Let's take an example of the kind of thing I feel I know best, like this piece of wax I have in front of me. I can see it, smell it, taste it, feel it, bang it with my hand and listen to the sound it makes. What could be better known? But when I put it by the fire, *all* those sensory properties change. Of course, it's still the same piece of wax – it's just melted. So what does that mean about the thing I knew? In itself, it can't have been any of those sensory properties, because they're gone, and *the thing itself* is still there (30).

So the wax wasn't any of those properties; it was just *a body*, which had those properties, but doesn't have them now. And what does that mean? What's a body? Something three-dimensional, whose parts can move relative to one another, and which can have different properties at different times. But that flexibility and change-ability isn't itself something I know through being able to picture it because the same body could take on many more different forms than I can picture. And many more different sizes. So my knowledge of what the wax really is in itself has all along been not something sensory or image-based, but something purely intellectual. At first that intellectual grasp of it was confused, and muddled up with the different images I have of it at different times; but now I see more clearly how I know it through *an intellectual interpretation* of those sensory data (30–1).

We talk as if we see objects with our eyes, when in reality we apprehend them with our intellects on the basis of the images our eyes provide – just as we say we see people passing by in the street, when all we really *see* is their hats and coats (31–2).

Obviously, when I first looked at the wax and knew it just through my senses, I understood it less well than I do now. Then I had an animal-like awareness of it; now I have the kind of grasp that only a human mind is capable of (32).

So it turns out that I know myself much better than I do objects around me. Because experience provides me only with *evidence* for the existence of things around me, but it provides *proof* that I exist to perceive them. And if I know objects better when I have more evidence for them, then I must know myself far better, because *every* experience I have gives knowledge of myself (33).

So now I know that objects aren't perceived by the senses, but only by the mind; and the mind is better known than any object is. I'd better stop there and get used to that discovery before I go on (34).

Commentary

As we have seen, The Thinker of the *Meditations* starts her inquiries by deliberately emptying her mind: by the Method of Doubt she sweeps away all her preconceived ideas and takes on the project of rebuilding the house of knowledge from the ground up [3.1.2]. In that way Descartes tries to demonstrate that his position needs no special training or background assumptions, but must be accepted by any rational person who looks at these questions honestly and objectively. But here's a question: is it really possible to do philosophy in this honest, open way? Can we really answer these questions without any philosophical commitments or theoretical presuppositions, or is Descartes just pulling the wool over our eyes? Is he really just *hiding* his philosophical allegiances, and letting us feel we are being open-minded only because we happen to share many of his prejudices?[23]

That question arises here because although this section doesn't take The Thinker's project forward very far, it is important in that in two areas – his metaphysics of matter, and his theory of mind – it reveals something of the bigger philosophical picture Descartes is trying to lead us towards.

1. Metaphysics of matter

Notice how Descartes says a physical object consists ultimately just of extended material stuff (26). What gives the wax all its properties, he says, is not some essential waxiness that it possesses, but just the fact that at the microscopic and submicroscopic level the matter that makes it up is arranged in such a way as to make it behave in certain ways and not in others. For Descartes, that is basically a *mechanical* process. For example, the bits of matter on the surface of the wax are so arranged that they reflect streams of light with a particular kind of speed and spin. And when light particles vibrating in just that way impact on our eyes, we have the experience of seeing something yellow [3.2.4; 3.2.5].

Nowadays, of course, we have a much more sophisticated account of the process. But the basic structure of contemporary accounts is still very Cartesian, isn't it? Most people take it for granted that all the observable properties of objects are a result of the way the object is put together at the atomic level, and of the way an atomic structure of that kind interacts with our nervous systems. Descartes offers no real argument for that view in the *Meditations*. Rather, the *Meditations* is intended to show that the kind of thinking he employs in getting to that picture – what we might call scientific thinking – is the only way to objective knowledge, and is perfectly compatible with orthodox Christianity.

Notice that the mechanical properties which matter really does have on this kind of account – the sizes, shapes, positions and motions of its constituent parts – are also properties that can be given precise *mathematical* values. Descartes thinks that while our sensory knowledge of the world is good for getting around in it, the only really accurate description of matter is a mathematical one, in which the sensory description of objects colliding is replaced by an equation stating the redistribution of numerical values involved. That description is the one that the man of science tries to achieve and is the closest we can manage to God's atemporal, non-sensory understanding of creation [3.3.9; 3.6.1].

2. Mind and knowledge

The second and more striking lesson of the Piece of Wax concerns Descartes' theory of perception, and what that shows us about his theory of mind.

According to Descartes, you don't really see objects at all. Or feel them, or smell them or sense them in any way. Of course, we *talk* as though we do – I say I *see* the monster on the bedpost, and I *feel* its breath on my neck – but actually I don't do anything of the kind. That's because perception is actually a *two-stage* process: I feel the *sensations* of sight and touch that the monster gives me, and I *work out*, on the basis of those sensations, that there is a monster on the bedpost, or whatever it might be. Strictly speaking, all I really *see* is light sensations; all I really *feel* is touch sensations. Of course it's true that without those sensations I would have no knowledge of the monster at all; but those sensations on their own aren't enough to give me such knowledge (they are 'necessary', but not 'sufficient' for me to know it's there) because I also need the ability to *interpret* those sensations: to recognize them, compare them with others, past and present, and to understand what they *mean* {OR6, 436–8}.

Is that true? Is such an 'Indirect Realist' story an accurate account of the way we perceive?

How does Descartes try to persuade us that it is?

There seem to be two, interconnected reasons in this section.

First, in the case of the wax, everything we get from our senses changes, yet the wax remains the same. So the wax itself can't be something we perceive with our senses.

Does that work?

Of course, other things we perceive aren't as changeable as the wax: it's very unusual for something to change *all* its sensory properties in a short time like that. (How convenient that it happened to be what came to hand when The Thinker was looking for an example of a physical object.) But the case can perhaps be generalized. Isn't it, in general, true that the way an object looks and feels (and the rest) can change, and it still remain the same thing? Indeed, that seems to be one of the things it means to be an *object*. (A patch of green couldn't change its colour and still be a patch of green; a patch of grass could change its colour and still be a patch of grass.)

Second, Descartes says the true nature of the wax isn't knowable in sensory terms. After all, the wax can take on an unthinkable, perhaps even an infinite, number of shapes. (Think about it. Melt the wax in a pan, and throw it around the room. What shape will it be when it sets? How many different shapes could it take on if you kept repeating the experiment?) We can *understand* that it has all those possibilities, but we can't *picture* them all.

Again, wax is a good example to make the point. But isn't the same true of *any* object? How many different shapes could the Taj Mahal take on if you ground it up into powder and dropped it from an aircraft on a windy day? Of course, you might say it wouldn't still *be* the Taj Mahal then – you would have destroyed it in the course of your experiment. But that's the point: *what it really is* is just the stuff that makes it up and which at the moment happens to have that particular, famous shape, colour, and so on [3.2.9].

For Descartes, this theory of perception is part of a much bigger picture of the nature of human beings and of their minds. Having sensations and responding to them he thinks is a physical, mechanical process which any animal with an appropriately sensitive body, or even a cleverly constructed robot, can do. Being *conscious* of those sensations, on the other hand, and being able to recognize and interpret them so as to construct a mental model of the world and of our own selves within it as beings with a past and a future – all that, he thinks, can't be explained by any kind of mechanical process. The ability to do those things shows there is more to human beings than the matter that makes them up: in addition to our bodies we have minds, or selves, which monitor and interpret our sensory states and consider our long-term goals and intentions.

We'll look at Descartes' 'dualistic' account of human life later [3.2.6]. For the moment, consider this question: does the 'Indirect Realist', two-stage account of perception we have just seen really make sense if we abandon the theory of mind that underpins it?

***

Meditation 2 hasn't developed The Thinker's quest very far, but it has laid some important foundations. She thinks she has shown:

1. That she can't doubt her own existence. So she *has* found something that is absolutely certain, and the Sceptical doubts of Meditation 1 are relieved at least to that extent.
2. That her knowledge of the world around her isn't simply given to her by her sensory experiences of it, but has to be

worked out by her active mind *on the basis* of her sensations, which are all that her senses actually provide.

Convinced?

Links

- Descartes' mechanistic account of nature is set out in 3.2.4.
- Descartes' 'dualist' account of human life is set out in 3.2.6 and 3.6.1.

3.2.4 DISCUSSION 6

MECHANISM: DESCARTES' BIG IDEA, AND THE JOB OF THE *MEDITATIONS*

The *Meditations* is perhaps Descartes' most famous work. And his most famous ideas are undoubtedly the epistemology and metaphysics he put into it, and into other works like the *Discourse* and the *Principles*. But those facts would have been both a surprise and a disappointment to Descartes himself. What he wanted and expected to be known for was for ideas which are not very prominent in the *Meditations*: his work in Physics. Quite simply, he thought he was the first person (in the Modern era, at least) to work out the true structure of the universe, and the mechanical principles according to which it operates.[24]

The relation of the *Meditations* to that ambition is indirect. It is the product of the new, more cautious approach he adopted after he abandoned his *magnum opus*, *The World*, on hearing of the condemnation of Galileo by the Inquisition [Chapter 1].[25] What does he have to do if he is to get his message across? He wants to show that the old, Aristotelian methods based on the collection and classification of appearances can tell us nothing, and have to be replaced by the rational analysis of those appearances, which will reveal the mathematically describable reality which underlies them [3.1.11]. But at the same time he needs to make clear that this new way of knowing the world is perfectly compatible with – and in fact strengthens – the Christian faith and the position of the Catholic Church. What he needs, therefore, is a treatise which shows that:

1. The only things we can really be certain of are not the way the world looks and feels to us, but our rational judgements [3.1.4].

2. Although it seems otherwise, *all* our knowledge of the world around us is actually arrived at by the rational interpretation of our sensory data [3.2.3].
3. Accepting the new Physics, far from leading us to abandon the Church's teachings and adopt a materialist account of human beings, actually proves to us the immateriality and therefore the immortality of the soul [3.2.6].
4. Far from leading to atheism, the new science proves the existence of God, and demonstrates that only the Christian can have an objective understanding of nature [3.4.1].

And so he wrote the *Meditations* in a traditional, religious format and with a dedication to the Learned Fathers of the Sorbonne – but in reality aimed at appealing over their heads (while keeping under their radar) to the kind of intelligent, unbiased readers that Descartes thought the Learned Fathers generally were not [3.1.1].

So what is the world really like, according to Descartes? What is the Big Idea that he intended to present openly in *The World*, and ended up preparing the ground for in the *Meditations*?

The answer is Mechanism. Descartes thought all the natural phenomena of the universe – the motions of the stars, the formation of the earth, the wings of a flea, the birth of a child – are just that: they are phenomena, appearances. They are *real* things and events, of course, but they are not the *basic* realities of the world, only ways in which those basic realities show themselves. And what are the basic, underlying realities which generate those phenomena? The answer is a single *continuum* of matter, the parts of which operate on each other in accordance with three simple mechanical *laws*. With the single exception of the actions of intelligent beings, everything that happens in the universe is the result of the ways in which the different regions of that material continuum rub, push, press, rattle and bang together.

Strange though it may seem, then, Descartes sees the whole material universe as a single object, a seamless, unbroken *continuum* of stuff which fills – indeed constitutes – the whole of space and everything it contains. But what about all the individual things in the world? The answer is that in reality they are not individual things at all, only different areas of that extended mass, individuated by the different ways in which they move.

Think about it. Why do we say that my bucket is one thing, and my spade is another? Only because the parts of the bucket are arranged in such a way that you can't (without a hacksaw) move one of them without moving the others, whereas you can very easily take the bucket home and leave your spade on the beach. And what about the space between and around them? In reality it isn't an empty *space* at all: it too is full of matter, the parts of which move past each other very easily – we call it 'air'; but it isn't nothing, and it isn't some essentially different stuff from the objects it surrounds. It's just the same extended matter, differently arranged.[26]

The *properties* of that matter are all in the end reducible to the mechanical properties of size, shape, position and motion [3.2.5]. And each of those properties can be stated as a *number*,[27] so that in theory the whole world can be described in non-sensory, mathematical terms.

The *laws* which govern the behaviour of material substance are very simple.

1. No part of matter moves unless it is pushed by another, or stops unless it is stopped by another. (What we call the law of 'inertia'.)
2. All parts of matter move in a straight line, unless deflected by other parts. (Straight-line motion.)
3. When two parts of matter collide, the sum total of motion they possess after the collision will be the same as before it, though it will be differently distributed (The 'conservation' of motion.) {*Principles*, 2.37–40}.

And by the combination of that material continuum with those three laws, Descartes claims nothing less than to offer an outline explanation of every natural event. Which is why I say he would be disappointed to be remembered only for his contributions to epistemology.

Atoms and the void: Two questions about our world-view

Descartes' Mechanism is a clear ancestor of modern-day physical theories. But two features of the world-view that most of us nowadays take for granted are things that Descartes explicitly denied: the existence of atoms, and of vacuums.

Most people nowadays assume an Atomist picture of the world: that all the phenomena of nature are in the final analysis to be explained by reference to the nature and behaviour of the parts that make them up, and that if we continue the process of dividing up objects long enough we will come down in the end to the fundamental, irreducible particles – whether they be called atoms, subatomic particles or whatever – that make up the whole of nature. ('The fundamental building-blocks of Nature.') Descartes argued that such irreducible particles were impossible.

Similarly, most people now seem to believe in the existence of vacuums: that in the space at the top of a Torricellian barometer, or in the Interstellar Void, there are areas of nothingness – mere empty space, with literally *nothing* in it. Descartes argued that vacuums are an absurdity.

Here are two Cartesian reasons for thinking that he is right, and we are wrong. What do you think?

1. However small a fundamental particle may be, it will continue to have *some* size or other. But that means we can ask questions about its internal organization: what connects the right-hand side to the left-hand side, for example? Is it solid, or not? If those questions make sense, then surely the particle is *not* after all a fundamental one, because its nature and behaviour are determined by its internal organization – by its *parts*. The fundamental elements of matter turn out to be not these particles, but the parts of those particles; the fundamental particles are themselves further divisible – not perhaps in practice (they're too small to chop up), but at least in thought. And of course, what applies to this particle will apply all over again to any of its parts. As Descartes says, because space is divisible to infinity, you can never reach a stopping-point of explanation by reducing things to smaller and smaller parts, so an atomist ontology is indefensible (*Principles*, 2.20).

2. If you have two things – such as the opposite sides of a box – and there is *literally nothing* between them, doesn't that mean they are in contact? Perhaps you think not, and you could have a box (or an interstellar space) with a vacuum in it. And then your box would contain nothing. How large would that nothing be? It seems like a strange question.

How can you measure nothing? But it would have to make sense, because if I also had a box with a vacuum in it, and my box was bigger than yours, then my nothing would be bigger than your nothing. So I couldn't put my nothing in your box, because it wouldn't fit. (Even though there was nothing in it.) Is that really a coherent story (*Principles*, 2.18)?

You can perhaps *make* it coherent if you think of space as Absolute – if you think of it as a kind of giant container, in which all the objects in existence are located. Then you can say that some parts of your container are occupied, and some are not – and those are the vacuums. That seems to me to be quite a high price to pay.

One final thought. It is not at all clear that contemporary physicists any longer believe in the existence of either atoms or the Void (vacuums). If your fundamental particles are not in fact particles at all, but non-localized wave-particle dualities which are smeared out across the entire universe (including the vacuums), then perhaps you are closer to a Cartesian picture than it seems.

Links

- For the place of the *Meditations* in Descartes' overall project, see Chapter 1.
- The metaphysics of Descartes' mechanism, and its relation to the question of Objectivity, both come up in 3.6.5.

3.2.5 DISCUSSION 7

'PRIMARY' AND 'SECONDARY' QUALITIES: SUBJECTIVITY AND THE ABSOLUTE VIEW

Why are woolly jumpers so tickly? When you wear them, they make you itch all the time. Do you think it's because wool is somehow imbued with a special quality of tickliness which other materials don't have? If so, I wish someone would invent a way of taking it out, and leaving us with clothes that both keep you warm and are comfortable to wear.

But of course, it doesn't work like that. Tickliness isn't a separate quality, like a separate ingredient that some things have and some things lack. To say that wool is tickly is just to say that the fibres of wool have a particular kind of fineness and stiffness, which put together mean that when it comes into contact with sensitive human skin it produces tickly sensations. You can't take the tickliness out of wool and leave the wool behind, the way you can take the air out of water by boiling it. It isn't a separate property, so to take away the tickliness you'd have to change the *other* properties of the wool: stick all the fibres together in some way, or coat them with some slippery stuff or something. In fact, you could achieve exactly the same result by leaving the wool alone, and injecting all the people with a special skin hardener, so that they ended up with hides like hippos. If you did that, then hey presto, all the jumpers would lose their tickliness – which just goes to show that it was never just a property of the wool, but a fact about how wool feels to *people*.

A silly example, you may think. (It's based on a version that Descartes uses in *The World*, XI.5–6). But the point is important. Tickliness, you might say, is not a separate property of things, in addition to the other properties they possess: it's just a fact about how those other properties typically affect human beings. We talk as if it were a property of wool that it is tickly, but in reality it's a fact about its interaction with *us* – that we are tickled by it. In the same way, dangerousness is not really a property which is shared by tigers, sharp knives and fast-moving traffic, but is just a slightly misleading way of expressing the fact that all of those things are capable of harming *people*.

Is that making sense? In general, we can separate out what we might call a thing's *inherent* properties – those which really are properties of the thing in question, and which it would have irrespective of how it was placed or who was dealing with it – from facts about the ways in which objects which have those inherent qualities consequently look and feel (etc.) to us. The former are generally referred to (using terminology which dates back to the seventeenth century) as *Primary Qualities*, and the latter are *Secondary Qualities*.

If you've got a grip of that basic idea, then ask yourself this question: where do the Secondary Qualities (facts about how we experience objects) end, and the Primary Qualities (facts about the objects themselves) begin?

In addition to tickliness and dangerousness, it's pretty clear that if we describe something as having a sweet taste, or as smelling like apples, for example, we will be listing some of its *Secondary* Qualities. Terms like those describe *how we are affected* by the object, rather than how it is in itself. (I'm not saying it's not *true* that sugar is sweet, any more than I'm saying that wool is not tickly; only making clear what its truth consists in.) Colour words are also famous examples of *Secondary* Qualities: to say that something is puce is to say that the inherent qualities of its surface are such that in normal light conditions it looks puce to people with normal eyesight.

So what would be examples of *Primary* Qualities, then?

Earlier on I said that the tickliness of wool depends on facts like the stiffness and fineness of its fibres. So are stiffness and fineness Primary Qualities?

Not really. Fineness is surely a *relative* property: to say that something is fine in this sense is to say that it's fine *relative to the sort of thing people usually compare it to.* If we were tiny, microscopic creatures that lived in wool, we'd see its fibres as being as fat and solid as tree trunks, and would laugh (with our tiny, inaudible laughs) if anyone described them as being fine and delicate. And the same is true of stiffness: stiffness (in this case) is the property of being relatively difficult to bend. But the stiffness of a wool fibre is nothing when compared to the stiffness of a book cover, and probably the hippos would laugh (with their huge, echoing guffaws) to hear us use the word 'stiff' for either of them. If a thing's fineness or stiffness is a function of who happens to be thinking about it, they are surely Secondary Qualities. So where are the Primary Qualities?

What we are looking for is those properties of a thing which don't involve reference to anything other than the thing itself. Tickliness, dangerousness, taste, colour, fineness and stiffness all fail that test because in various ways they relate not just to the object, but to its interactions with people. What properties *don't* have that feature?

For Descartes, the list of Primary Qualities was usually size, shape, position and motion (*Principles*, 4.187). What is *inherent* in a wool fibre (or any other material object), what it is *in itself*, what *makes it what it is*, is just the way the matter that constitutes it is arranged. So the Primary Quality which underlies what we know as the fineness of wool fibres is their having a mean thickness of 0.03 mm, or something of the kind; and that which explains its stiffness is the way the parts of it are interconnected, which results in its bending under a pressure of so many grams.

Does that make sense? Descartes sees those particular properties as Primary because of his Mechanism [3.2.4]: if we are going to explain the world mechanically, as a consequence of the various ways in which the different parts of matter rub, push, press and bang together, then the properties we are going to take as fundamental in an object are the shapes, sizes, motions and positions of its parts. (And if we are going to explain the world mathematically, those mechanical properties will be stated as numerical values.)

Nowadays, of course, we have a more sophisticated Physics, and so our list of Primary Qualities might be rather different: we might decide that electrical charge, for example, is an irreducible feature of a material object which we need to refer to in order to explain its observable properties, in which case we would say that charge is a Primary Quality, and so on. The essential points to grasp are these:

1. Most people nowadays would agree with Descartes in thinking that there is a natural and important distinction between Primary and Secondary Qualities.
   - We would probably disagree with him about the details of what to put on each list, but agree that such lists can be made.
   - This is true even though most people have never heard of the distinction. For most of us it's just part of the unspoken, unrecognized set of philosophical assumptions which structure the various ways in which we understand the world around us [3.2.9].
2. Accepting the distinction means accepting that many of the properties that in ordinary speech we attribute to objects are not in fact features of the objects as they are in themselves, but of how they are in relation to us.
   - The way a thing is for us derives from, or is explained by, both the way it is in itself *and* the way we deal with it.

3. It would therefore in theory be possible to give a complete description of an object by listing only its Primary Qualities.
   - What that complete description would give us is a purely objective, impersonal account of the thing in question: the object as a perfect science would know it.
4. In Descartes' day this distinction, which we now take for granted, was a radical new invention which had to be argued for.
   - Philosophical orthodoxy at the time made no such distinction. A thing's colour, for example, would be regarded as a property of it in just the same way as its size [3.1.11].

If all that is true, it seems to me that two questions arise for anyone who wants to understand the position Descartes is taking.

1. Are there really any Primary Qualities?
   (a) Take, for example, the property of being 3 m long. Is that a separate property from the property of being three times as long as a metre rule? Or the property of tending to be held to be 3 m long by people who have measured it? Both of those properties seem to be Secondary Qualities. What remains of the length if you take those away?
   (b) According to Einstein, a thing's size is not a Primary Quality at all, but a function of the relative speed of the object and the observer. If size and shape aren't Primary, what is?
   (c) In general, is it true that we can strip away from our conception of the world all the properties which have a relation to us, and still be left with any meaningful account of it? Will what we are left with be an Objective view, or no view at all [3.6.5]?
2. For Descartes, the distinction makes perfect sense because it is part of his 'dualist' account of human experience [3.2.6]. The Primary Qualities are the real properties of the object – the object as God knows it, and as the pure human intellect knows it – and the Secondary Qualities are the way it feels to an embodied human mind. The task of science (and of religion, and of morality [3.3.9]) is to escape from

the misleading impressions of the latter and try as far as possible to know the world purely intellectually. In that way we not only see the world as it really is, but we recapitulate in our own small way God's non-sensory understanding of his creative activity. If we take away all that metaphysical and psychological underpinning from the distinction, why would we want to maintain it?

Links

- Descartes' mechanism is set out in 3.2.4.
- His 'dualism' is set out primarily in 3.2.6.
- The wider metaphysical question of which that of Primary and Secondary Qualities is a part is asked in 3.6.5.

3.2.6 DISCUSSION 8

CARTESIAN 'DUALISM': MONISM, PLURALISM AND DUALIST LIFE

One of the most famous aspects of Descartes' philosophy is his Dualism – his belief in the essential separateness of Mind and Body. Textbooks on the Philosophy of Mind all start with 'Cartesian Dualism' (and often make no attempt to understand what Descartes actually thought). Yet in an important sense, Descartes is not a dualist at all.

A *mon*ist in ontology [3.2.9] is someone who thinks there is only *one* substance – that despite appearances to the contrary, everything that exists is in reality just a part or an aspect or a manifestation of a single thing. Spinoza is a monist in just that sense. A *dual*ist, therefore, should be someone who thinks that there are *two* substances in existence. But Descartes doesn't think that. In a slightly different sense, you might say a monist is someone who believes there is only one *kind* of substance. That would have the odd consequence of meaning that even Leibniz, despite his avowed *plural*ism (he believed that every cell in your body, and every one of the infinitesimally small subcells that make it up, was a separate substance created expressly by God) would have to be called a monist. And to say that Descartes was a dualist in that sense would suggest he believed that there are many minds and many bodies, all of them substances of two different *kinds*. But he didn't think that, either.

So what *did* he think? And why does everyone call him a dualist?

Descartes' ontology is a curious kind of hybrid. In the *material* world, he is (despite some looseness in his terminology) a straightforward monist: he thinks that God made only one material object, which is the single extended mass which constitutes the material universe. All the 'individuals' within that mass are only modes of that one substance – regions of the whole, which are conventionally individuated on the basis of relative motion, and can be destroyed if they are broken up and the motions that identify them are redistributed [3.2.4]. In the *mental* world, though, the picture is completely different. Individual minds are emphatically *not* just aspects or areas of a single mental continuum. Each one is a separate thinking substance, 'really distinct' [3.6.2] from every other; each one is expressly created by God, and is incapable of being destroyed unless God chooses to annihilate it. In the mental world, in other words, Descartes is an out-and-out Pluralist.

All a bit of a mess, really. And a factor which inclines some people to think that the belief in the existence of immortal souls, like the belief in God, is just a sop to the authorities, bolted on to a straightforwardly naturalistic theory [3.3.9].

So, if Descartes is a material monist and a mental pluralist, why is he always known as a dualist? The answer (if we discount a certain amount of sloppy thinking around the fact that he allows existents of two different kinds) is that he gives a radically *dualistic* account of human beings, and of human life.

1. Cartesian physiology

First, a bit of background. What is the difference between a dead person and a living one? Sometimes it can be very hard to tell them apart. At least for a time after death a dead person looks just the same as a living one; and even if you chop them up you won't find anything that living people have and dead ones don't. Observationally, from the point of view of experience, the only difference is that living people typically do things that dead people don't – things like breathing, eating, moving around, speaking, picking their noses and watching TV. Typically, I think you will agree, living people are much more *animated* than dead ones.

The word 'animated', of course, is linked to the Latin word 'anima', which is roughly equivalent to the English word 'soul'. And it seems that when Aristotle said that the difference between plants and stones is that plants have a vegetative 'soul', he meant no more than the simple observational claim that plants tend to do things that stones don't, like feed, grow, change with the seasons and reproduce themselves. And when he said that *anima*ls ('anima' again) differ from plants in also possessing an animal soul, he meant no more than that animals can do all those things, but also behave in ways that plants don't, primarily in moving around. And so when he also said that people have a third, rational, soul, he again meant no more than the simple descriptive claim that people when they are alive do things that animals don't, such as speaking, reasoning, and thinking about what they *should* do.

By the time of Descartes, though, Aristotle's descriptive, biological account had been lost and found, corrupted, amended, Christianized and used to support a dying intellectual and political system; so it was very far from the system Aristotle had originally devised. In particular (and I'm now coming round to the point I'm supposed to be talking about), people were tending to give the term 'soul' a kind of explanatory role which Aristotle had never envisaged: they were saying that people could think and read books *because* they had a rational soul, and that the reason dead people can't watch TV is *because* their souls have left their bodies – which in Aristotelian terms is about as helpful as saying that people can think because they can think, and that living people are alive because they are living. The soul, in other words, had come to be thought of not as a characteristic pattern of behaviour, but as a separate *thing*, which *causes* people to behave in characteristic ways. (The soul has been 'reified' or 'hypostatized'.)

Descartes himself sketches this view in Meditation 2, where he has The Thinker say she'd always taken the soul to be 'something tenuous (*exiguum/rare et subtile*), like a wind or fire or ether, which permeated my more solid parts', and which explains

69

why she eats, moves, perceives and thinks (26). But the first thing to grasp about Cartesian Dualism is that although Descartes does say we each have an individual thinking soul, he thinks this debased Aristotelian theory is completely wrong.

So what does Descartes think explains the difference between living people and dead ones? The same as explains the difference between a fridge that works and one that doesn't. The human body is a mechanical robot. Its life is not the mysterious product of an animating wind or fire, but just the fact that the parts of this hugely complex organism are operating on one another to produce their usual effects. The organism grows, for example, because food is broken down in the stomach and intestines into smaller particles, some of which are distributed around the body, primarily by the circulating blood, and gradually accumulate in the limbs and organs so as to cause them to enlarge. The organism seeks food when its fuel reserves drop. It is able to do so because it is sensitive to its environment; most obviously, light rays are focused by the lenses of the eyes to produce images of the world around it, by which it is able to navigate. It moves by the expanding and contracting of muscles, and those expansions and contractions are caused by the incredibly rapid flow of particles along the nerves. When the organism is in danger – for example, when its hand comes into close contact with the very energetic particles of a fire, sensors in the skin trigger a flow of particles which cause the hand to pull away, the head to turn to see the cause of the problem, the legs to tense to carry it away from danger if necessary, and so on.

All that is true of the living human body, as it is true, with varying levels of complexity, of living animals. It is a very complex and sophisticated mechanism. And it is relatively easily broken up. If it suffers major external damage, the system breaks down, it no longer functions, and we say the person has been killed. In addition, over time the parts of the mechanism wear and begin to work less well, and eventually this process reaches the point where the whole system collapses, and we say the person has died of natural causes.[28]

If all that is true, then where does the soul come in? The simple answer is that Descartes says that *some* of the things human beings can do can't be explained in this way, and show that there is more to us than just a mechanical robot [3.2.8].

So much for the Cartesian body. What, then, of the Cartesian mind? Here are

2. *Ten things you need to know about the Cartesian soul or mind*

1. It isn't anywhere. Don't think of it as being in your head or behind your eyes or anywhere else in your body. It is no more in your body than it is in your wardrobe. It is an *immaterial* thing, wholly apart from the continuum of space, and therefore has *no* spatial coordinates. Remember, there are two kinds of thing in existence: matter, and also non-material, non-locatable but equally *real* things called minds or souls [3.2.8].

2. Although because it is immaterial it is not in any literal sense attached to your body, it is *sensitive* to its states. When, therefore, in my example above you put your hand too near to the fire, something else happens, in addition to the body's responses, which is that your mind is *aware* of your body's pain.

    The best way to make sense of that I think is like this. Imagine you had no memory beyond half a second ago. You would still be alive. You would still feel (very short) pains, pleasures and so on – you would see the sunset, smell the flowers, and all the rest. But you wouldn't know what a sunset *is*, because you can't recognize it as such without being aware of how this sensation relates to others you have had or could have, and to other things you know and have known in the past. More importantly, with a half-second memory you wouldn't even be *aware* of your sensations, you wouldn't be *conscious* of them – because you wouldn't be aware of any *change* in you. You wouldn't, while feeling the pain or whatever, simultaneously be aware of a previous, different state you had been in. You would therefore have no grasp of what pain *is*, because you would have no simultaneous conception of anything else. And more obviously, you would have no conception that *you* were in pain, because to have an awareness of something as happening to *you*, you need a conception of your*self* as a being that persists through time, and that undergoes different experiences.

Does that make sense? According to Descartes, we could say, the body has experiences, has sensations, because of its complex, sensitive structure. But I am only *conscious* of those states because a relationship exists between the part of the material world that is my body, and a separate, non-material entity which monitors its states. And that is my mind or soul [3.6.1].

3. In addition to providing *consciousness* of my body's states, my mind also *interprets* them. That is what we saw in the example of the piece of wax [3.2.3]. My body senses its environment, and my mind, because it monitors the body's states, is able to make inferences and to *understand* the world around it. So my body merely feels the heat of the fire; my mind is aware of that feeling, and judges that it is caused by a fire.

4. My mind therefore develops the *concept* of fire, an understanding of what fire is. That understanding can be crude and impressionistic, little more than a collection of memories and images; or it can be sophisticated and intellectual (if I have read enough Descartes to know about human physiology and the Physics of fires).

5. Because my mind has concepts, it can learn *language*: it can set up conventional relationships between certain sounds or shapes and the concepts it has acquired, and so can communicate with other people. That is something quite different from animal 'languages' which can be explained mechanically – as when a blackbird's alarm-call causes other blackbirds in the area to take flight, an aggressive shake of the antlers causes another stag to move away, or a frightened bleat causes a sheep to approach its lamb {*Discourse*, 6, VI.56–9}.

6. In addition to having awareness of my body's states, my mind is also aware of other things. It can think about the future, and the past beyond the reach of memory. It can think about abstractions, like mathematics, government, international development, the 12 tone scale and antidisestablishmentarianism. It can think about morality, and it can think about God.

7. All these different forms of awareness, from awareness of sensations to abstract thought, come under the heading

of *Perception* in Descartes' language. But *thinking*, which is what minds do, has two forms, of which Perception is only one. The other is *Willing*. My body can do things – seek food, run from danger, attack an enemy – but my mind can make *choices*. Whereas the actions of the body are the result of forces operating on it, so that the strongest force will always win out, the mind can sometimes overcome the body's cravings and act for other reasons – like not eating because you want to lose weight, or not sleeping with your boyfriend because you promised his granny you wouldn't {*Principles*, 1.32–42}.

8. How does the mind do these various things? *How* does it become aware of the body's states, and *how* does it influence the body's actions? This, sometimes known as the Problem of Interaction, is one of the most written-about features of the system, and many people think it renders the whole story implausible.

In a sense there is no answer to the question, if what we are looking for is some *mechanical* or other *physical* process.[29] For as long as you are alive, there is a two-way relation of awareness and influence between your physical body and your non-physical mind. The process has no stages or mechanisms; it is immediate and unmediated. Just as you can give no *further* explanation for the way in which one moving object causes another to move (you can explain how quickly or how slowly it moves, and in what direction, but you can't say any more about *why* it happens – it's just what solid objects do when they meet), so also you can give no further explanation of how minds and bodies interact: it's just what they do {*Principles*, 4.197}.

9. The body doesn't die because the soul leaves it. On the contrary, the soul 'leaves' because the body is dead. Death, as we have seen, is a physical process with physical causes. When the body ceases to function, the relationship between it and the soul is broken: the body no longer has the sensations of which the mind had been aware, and it is no longer capable of responding to the mind's decisions (*Passions*, 1.6).

10. The death of the body, therefore, has no effect at all on the mind, other than to change its experiences. It loses the window on the physical world which its relationship with

the body had provided; and it becomes free from the misleading appearances and non-rational urgings which that relationship had subjected it to. But in itself it is unchanged by the change. The soul itself cannot die, because death is a physical process, the breakup and breakdown of a material organism. But the mind is not a material thing, and has no parts which can break down or fall apart. So the mind is immortal (Synopsis of *Meditations*, 13–14).

That, then, is Cartesian Dualism: not a dualist ontology, but a radically dualist, divided account of human life. A living person is not one thing, but two: physical and non-physical, lower and higher, earthly and divine. It is a picture which still dominates our attitudes in areas like religion and morality, but also I think in psychology, epistemology, metaphysics and also politics, where it is intimately bound up with the notions of individuality and individualism. More importantly for our purposes, it forms the whole basis of Descartes' attempt to solve what I have called the Problem of Objectivity [Chapter 2]. Is Cartesian Dualism true? If not, can you solve the Problem of Objectivity without it?

Links

- The idea of ontology is set out in 3.2.9.
- Descartes' argument for the separation of Mind and Body is considered in 3.2.8.
- There is more on how the two are related in 3.6.1.

3.2.7 DISCUSSION 9

IS THERE A SELF? (1): THE *COGITO*, LICHTENBERG, AND THE POSSIBILITY OF ONTOLOGY

I said in the Commentary on Section 3.2.2 that if the *Cogito* works, then it proves very little – not the existence of *me*, the person I know myself to be, with my body and personality and history and interests and so on, but just this thinker, the thing – whatever it is – that's having these present thoughts [3.2.2]. But does it really prove even that much?

It is clear at the beginning of Meditation 2 that there is 'thinking' going on. There is doubting. There is the asking and answering of questions. If there is a Malicious Demon behind it all then that thinking is mistaken, certainly; but there has to be thinking in order even for there to be mistakes. But does the admitted fact that there is *thinking* going on really mean that there has to be a *thinker*?

The question is always associated with the philosopher and physicist Georg Lichtenberg.[30] He compared thinking to lightning: when we see there is lightning going on, we don't assume there has to be a lightner, so why should we conclude that if there is thinking then there has to be a thinker?

What do you think? Are the two cases the same?

Some people object that although Lichtenberg is right that we don't jump from lightning to the existence of a lightner, we *do* jump to the existence of *something* that underlies the lightning. Perhaps lightning is a flash from the hammer of Thor; perhaps it's the trail of an alien spaceship; perhaps it's charged particles produced by clouds; but whatever it is, there is *something* behind it – there can't be lightning unless there is *something that is doing* the lightning, can there?

Let's be clear what the problem is here. The question is not whether there must be some *cause* of the lightning – something that makes it happen, or some preceding event that sets it off. It's rather a question of what the lightning *is*, in itself – what kind of *thing* it is. The event, the flash, occurs, that much is clear. So doesn't there have to be *something in which* it occurs? There can't just be an event; that event must happen *to* something; it must be a stage or a process or a set of happenings in the life of some *thing* (or things), mustn't it? This isn't a fact about lightning, it's a fact about events. Events can't just happen: there must be something they happen *to*.

The same line of thinking applies to properties. If there is yellow, then there must be some*thing* that is yellow. If there is useful, there must be some *thing* or *things* that is/are useful. And so on.

If that line of thought makes sense, then the case of the lightning is in fact very similar to the *Cogito*. Here, too, the idea is not that something must be *causing* my thinking – something must set off my train of thought, or make me think this way.

(That may be true, but it isn't what drives the *Cogito*.) The point is rather that if there is thinking going on, then there must be *something in which* it is going on. There can't just be acts of thinking, as it were floating around on their own; if there is an act of thinking, then there must be something that is *performing* that act of thinking. Acts need agents, just as events need things they go on in, and properties need things they are properties of.

So far, then, so good for Descartes. We seem to have fought off the Lichtenberg objection by arguing that thinking can't be going on unless there is something it is going on *in*, or something that's doing it. But this raises another question, which I suspect is in fact the real point that Lichtenberg was trying to make. The question is simply this: *why* are we convinced that events, actions and properties can't exist on their own? Do we have some argument for it, or is it just some kind of deep-seated prejudice?

This question goes really deep. *Why* do we have this conviction that there can't be an instance of pink unless there is some*thing* that is pink? That there can't be thinking unless there is a thinking *thing*? What we run up against here is our basic ontology [3.2.9]: most of us take it for granted that the universe is a universe of *things*, and that everything else we take to exist – properties, events, actions, processes, and so on – can't exist on their own, but exist only in virtue of the existence of *things*. And the question is, where does that belief come from? *Why* do we have an ontology of objects?

This is the question that arises in the analysis of the *Cogito* [3.2.1]: does the *Cogito* only work if Descartes assumes the extra premise that all thinkers are existers, and if so, is he entitled to that assumption? As I said there, his answer is in effect that unless you know that thinking is a mental *act*, something a thinking *thing* does, then you don't know what thinking is. It is, therefore, something that is presupposed by the *Cogito*. But he says that doesn't mean it's an extra premise, only that you need to know what 'think' means (as well as 'I' and 'therefore' and 'am') before you can accept it.

Does that seem right? Is our conviction that the universe is a universe of *things* a necessary truth, something we have to take for granted if we are to think intelligibly at all? Or is it just a *theory* we happen to hold, something we all take for granted, but which needs some argument if the belief is to be justified?

The question is too big to be settled here, but here is a line of thought to get you started.

Could it be that the belief that the universe consists in the end of *objects* of some kind (perhaps ordinary objects, like people and planets; perhaps tiny objects, like atoms and subatomic particles; perhaps a single object, like Descartes' material continuum [3.2.4]) is not, as it seems to be, a deep truth about how the world is, but just a function of our *language*. English, like most Indo-European languages, is a language with nouns, verbs and adjectives. To say anything at all, to *think* anything at all, in English, is to say or think that something does something, or something is some way and not another – the sun is shining, the vomit is green, and so on. Is that because our language is naturally attuned to the structure of nature? That because we find ourselves in a world of objects, it is natural for us to structure our language around words – nouns – which refer to those objects, and then to talk about how they are, and what they do? Or could it be the other way around – that because we happen to speak a language of nouns, we automatically and unthinkingly represent the world in the categories that our language provides, and so think of it as a collection of *things*? And when we do Metaphysics, and we think we are discovering deep truths about the Nature of Being, is all we are doing looking at ourselves in the mirror, and thinking we've seen something interesting and new?

Links

- The nature of ontology is explored further in 3.2.9, with a follow-up in 3.3.6.
- Descartes' ontology is set out in 3.2.4 and 3.2.6.

3.2.8 DISCUSSION 10

IS THERE A SELF? (2): DO I HAVE A MIND WHICH IS SEPARATE FROM MY BODY?

Let's assume that the *Cogito* works, and does allow us to be certain of our own existence [3.2.1]. Let's assume that means Lichtenberg is wrong: I don't just know there is thinking going on, I know there is some*thing* which is me – an I, a self of some kind yet to be established [3.2.7]. In the text above (25–6), The Thinker says to have a self is clearly more than just having a body because corpses have those; but at this stage she leaves open the possibility that her self depends on her body in some less obvious way. She doesn't return to the question until Meditation 6 [3.6.2], at which point she concludes that her self is quite separate from her body, and could exist without it.

The reason for the delay is that before Descartes can present us with his argument for the distinctness of mind and body he has to validate the kind of argument he is going to use – a process which isn't complete until Meditation 6. But because a grasp of the Cartesian self is so central a part of understanding the *Meditations* as a whole, I am going to look at the overall argument here, and consider the validation of arguments of that kind later on [3.4.1]. I've set out the kind of thing I think the Cartesian soul, mind or self is, and how I think it relates to the body, in 3.2.6. Here we are going to look at the question of whether there is any good reason for us to believe that the mind and the body are separate things.

But that question leads in many directions, and can't, it seems to me, be settled by a single, knock-down proof of the kind we will see that Descartes employed. So I am going to break it into four parts.

1. Can there be immaterial existents?
2. Is there more to a person than his/her body?
3. Could my mind exist without my body?
4. Could my mind exist without *any* body?

Descartes answers 'yes' to all those questions. What do *you* think?

1. Can there be immaterial existents?

This question is too big to answer here. I raise it only because the answer we want to give to it seems to me to underlie many people's reactions to the issue as a whole. Many people think Descartes is wrong, not because they can see something wrong with his arguments, but because they are convinced his conclusion is false, so there *must* be something wrong with either his premises or his reasoning (or both). And the reason we think his conclusion is false is because we can't accept the idea that there are immaterial things: how could there be these mental things just kind of floating around? Things which exist in time, but not in space; things which affect and are affected by things in the material world, but are no part of that world, and have no intelligible connection with it?

That seems to me a perfectly reasonable response to Descartes.[31] But we still need to think about the other four questions. And, if the answers you want to give to them are inconsistent with the answer you give to this one, you will have learned something.

But before we move on, ask yourself this question: *if* you think there are no immaterial existents, *why* do you think it? It seems to me to be an attitude, a picture, an ontology which most of us unthinkingly adopt: the universe just *is* all the material things it is made up of [3.2.9]. What it means to say that something is real is that it is one or more of those material things, or is in some way reducible to them, made up of them or produced by them. But do we have any good *reason* for that view, or is it just a prejudice we have inherited? Historically speaking this 'Materialist' outlook has been a minority view, which few thinkers have taken seriously. Do we have some argument to show that the majority have been wrong? Or is it just that we think it is true because we believe it – we are modern, we are advanced, we have insights into the world that previous generations have lacked. This is part of how we see things – so it *must* be true?

2. Is there more to a person than his/her body?

Try this thought experiment. Alien beings have come to earth. We don't notice them because they are very small, and they are not carbon-based life-forms. They would appear to us if we could detect them as small and constantly changing clouds of inert gas, smelling faintly of sick.

They are, though, extremely intelligent beings (or perhaps groups of beings: they seem constantly to merge and unite in novel and disturbing ways), and because of their small size and volatile nature they are able to penetrate and explore the gross, meaty lumps that we call human beings. They have chosen you as their particular object of study (if you sniff hard you might detect them), and over time they have built up a *perfect* knowledge of every cell in your body, and they are able to follow *perfectly* every event that happens in it – every chemical process, every electrical impulse – there is *nothing* they do not know about your body and what goes on in it. Question: Do these creatures (call them Wispas) know what you're thinking? Do they know how you feel? Do they know what it's like to be you?

It seems to me that they don't – that no amount of knowing which bits of my brain and body are doing what and when and how can ever *in itself* amount to a knowledge of my mental states.

The Wispas could only ever understand me or you if they are the right sort of thing – if they are near enough to people; if they can fall in love, feel lonely, embarrassed, frightened, proud and silly; if they can play games and be tempted to cheat; if they can be frightened and can die – *then* they may be able to do it because then they will perhaps be able to work out what kind of state of your body correlates with your being in those different conditions. But if they are not capable of at least a lot of those things (and lots of others), then their perfect knowledge of your physical make-up will tell them nothing at all about *you*, will it?

Is that true? If so, it seems to mean that there is more to me than what the Wispas know. And since they know everything there is to know about my body, that means there is more to me than my body, doesn't it? It may not be immaterial; it may not be an extra *thing*; it may be something my body does, or something it produces; but whatever that extra bit might be, it seems that a purely physical description of me would be seriously incomplete because it would leave out *me* altogether.

3. Could my mind exist without my body?

Assume for the moment that Descartes is wrong, and your mind has a purely physical basis. It isn't a separate, independent entity (a separate 'substance'), it's something your body produces, or something it does or in some other way it is a function of your material body.

Now, your body is just a collection of material parts. There is nothing magical or mysterious about it, no essential youness which gives rise to your distinctive personality and consciousness – it's just something about the way the matter that makes you up is arranged, and the way it has been modified over the years to produce your particular set of interests, memories, habits and so on, that results in your being the person you are, and having the 'mind' that you have.

It follows, doesn't it, that you are not identical with the particular bits of matter that happen to make you up. If every atom in your body were replaced by an identical one, while all its relations to all the other atoms that make you up were preserved, then you would be unaffected. (In fact, it is said that the natural processes of cell death and regeneration mean that on average every atom in your body is replaced every 7 years.) Indeed, if it were possible to produce a perfect record of every atom in your body at a given moment (perhaps the Wispas could do it), then it would in principle be possible to construct an exact replica of your body, and, therefore (given our assumptions), a *perfect* replica of your mind. But then your original body could be destroyed, yet your mind (or at least something identical to it in every respect) would live on in the new one, wouldn't it?

It seems to me to follow that if your mind *is* just a function of your body, then, paradoxical though it may seem, it follows that your mind could exist without your body. And of course, if (as Descartes thinks) your mind *isn't* just a function of your body, then the same conclusion will follow.

You might think that's cheating. That if my body is destroyed and I am re-created in a new one made out of recycled plastic cups, or something, then it's not that I exist without my body, but just that what I refer to as 'my body' has changed – it used to be *that* collection of bits which has now been ground up and fed to weasels, and now it's *this* collection of bits made out of old plastic cups. But the point is the same. Your mind can exist independently of any given collection of matter, and that includes the collection which at any given time you refer to as 'your' body.

4. *Could my mind exist without* **any** *body?*

This is the real issue that divides Cartesians from non-Cartesians. Descartes tries to show not only that your mind is something more than just your body, and not only that it is independent of any particular piece or pieces of matter, but also that it is an independently existing entity which is complete in itself, and would survive the destruction of *all* matter, and of all other created minds. (On the question of its relation to *God's* mind, see 3.2.6.) He tries to show it is a separate *substance* [3.2.9]. Is he right?

His argument for this begins in Meditation 2 [3.2.2], and is completed in Meditation 6 [3.6.2], and it goes something like this:

1. I can't doubt the existence of my self. (That's what the *Cogito* shows.)
2. I *can* doubt the existence of the whole material world. (We did that with the Dream Argument in Meditation 1.)
3. So the idea of my self doesn't involve the idea of anything physical.
4. So my self can't be part of the material world, and could exist without it.[32]

Does that work?

Many people have dismissed it on the grounds that it tries to derive a factual conclusion from psychological premises. What I can and can't doubt, they say, is a function of what I know, not of what there is (they think that because Descartes lived a long time ago and hadn't studied formal logic, he didn't realize that), and they give lots of alleged counterexamples along the lines of

1. I can't doubt that Anthony Trollope was Anthony Trollope.
2. I can doubt that Anthony Trollope was the inventor of the pillar-box.
3. Therefore, Anthony Trollope was not the inventor of the pillar-box.

But of course we all know that he was.

To say that, though, is to miss Descartes' point altogether. The point he is trying to make is not a psychological one, but a logical one, and is better represented as

1. Given that I am thinking, it is not logically possible that I don't exist.
2. It *is* logically possible, even given that I am thinking, that there is no material world.
3. Therefore, it is logically possible that I exist and the material world doesn't.
4. Therefore, I am something separate from the material world.

How does that strike you?

First we will look at whether the argument would work if the premises were true (whether it is 'valid'). Then we will ask whether it is reasonable to recast Descartes' psychological premises in this form, and then we'll look at whether the premises are actually true.

So is the argument valid? (If the premises are true, must the conclusion be true?)

Yes, it is. To say that it's not logically possible that I don't exist when I'm thinking is to say that the situation can never obtain: there can never be a situation in which I am thinking but don't exist, or there is no possible world in which I think but I don't exist. And to say it *is* logically possible that I think but matter doesn't exist is to say there *are* possible states of affairs, there are possible worlds, in which I am thinking, and there is no matter. But those two together mean that there are possible worlds in which I exist, and matter doesn't. (Some of those possible worlds contain no matter; all of them contain me; so there are some that contain me and no matter.) And that surely means that I am something separate from the material world because I could exist without it.

Agreed?

OK, so we have a valid argument to the conclusion that my self is separate from the material world. But Descartes doesn't write about logical possibility; is this a fair representation of his line of thought?

What he actually says is that the fact that he can't doubt himself but can doubt matter shows that he can 'Clearly and Distinctly conceive' of his mind separately from all thought of matter [3.3.1]. And what he has done between Meditation 2 and Meditation 6 is to satisfy himself that his Clear and Distinct Ideas must be true [3.4.1], which is why the argument gets delayed. As he puts it himself, if I can separate two things in thought, then God *could* separate them in reality {78; OR2, 169–70; OR6, 425} – that is, it is logically possible that one should exist without the other.

If that seems dubious, ask yourself: how do we know that it is not logically possible for a triangle not to have three sides, but it is logically possible for a triangle not to be green? The answer, surely, is that the concept of triangularity involves that of three-sidedness, but not that of greenness. And what does that mean but that, if you think about it carefully, you can see that you can't understand triangularity independently of three-sidedness? In Cartesian language, you Clearly and Distinctly conceive that they can't be separated.

The question of the relation between conceivability and necessity is a complex one, and I am not trying to settle it here, only to show how I think Descartes' argument was intended. If that is right, then it is not as crazy as has been thought, and can be represented as a valid argument for the conclusion that your mind could exist without *any* body. If we want to deny his conclusion, therefore, we will have to deny either premise 1 or premise 2. (Or both.) Can we do that?

To deny premise 1 is to deny the *Cogito*. If you were persuaded by that, then to avoid Descartes' conclusion you will have to deny premise 2 – that is, you will have to say that, although in Meditation 1 it seems as if we are able to doubt the existence of the whole material world and to envisage the possibility that all my apparent experience of it is some kind of illusion, that is not in fact so. And if you can't do that, then it seems to me that you will have to admit that your mind could (not *does*, but *could*) exist even if there were no matter, and therefore that it is a separate, non-material thing.

Personally, I prefer to deny premise 2.

Links

- The completion of the argument for the separation of mind and body comes in 3.6.2.
- The relation Descartes sees between Mind and Body is set out in 3.2.6, and you can see more of it in 3.6.1.
- The question of the relation of Dualism to Objectivity is raised in 3.6.5.

3.2.9 DISCUSSION 11

ONTOLOGY: SUBSTANCES AND MODES

Much of the excitement of Philosophy comes from discovering things you've always believed, but never thought about. It is the job of philosophers to become aware of those unexamined assumptions, and to find reasons to defend or reject them. The big advantage of reading the *History* of Philosophy is that you encounter people whose unexamined assumptions are different from our own, which enables us to see our own presuppositions more clearly.

Ontology is a case in point. Consider these three things: the shape of your head; Catherine the Great's coin collection; the Leaning Tower of Pisa (LTP). Do those things exist? Are they all real?

Surely they do, and they are. Your head isn't shapeless, so there must be such a thing as the shape of it. (It may not be any regular, recognizable shape, of course – it's unlikely to be a cube, or a tetrahedron, for example – but if you've got a head, it must have *some* shape or other.) Catherine's coin collection certainly exists – it's in the Hermitage Museum, apparently. And even the LTP, although it may look like some kind of bizarre fantasy, or a model made of icing sugar, is in fact a real building which you could climb up, fall off or blow up to get yourself on TV.

At the same time, though, these three things are surely very different, and although it would be crazy to say that any of them doesn't exist, it's not at all clear that they exist in the same way, or that when we say they are all real we are saying the same thing about each of them.

To say the LTP exists is to say that it's a real object, something to be met with in the world, a necessary constituent of any complete description of What There Is In Existence. The *shape* of something is surely very different from that. The shape of your head isn't a further, additional thing, over and above your head itself. (If I took a picture of your head, there would only be one thing in the picture, not two.) A thing's shape is surely just a property of it, an aspect of it, a way it is – not an *extra* thing in its own right.

What about the coin collection? Is that an extra existent, like your head or the LTP? Or is it just an aspect of something else?

Well, you might say it's not an extra thing because if you took away all the individual coins that make it up it would be gone, so it starts to look like the shape of your head: not a thing in itself, but a way of talking about the way some other things – the coins – are arranged. But on the other hand you could say the same about the LTP: it is surely just an aggregate of lots of bits of marble and stuff. Take all those away and there's no more LTP, is there?

There is a lot more you could say about just those simple examples. What I am trying to show with them is two things:

1. that we all unthinkingly take for granted a distinction between things and their properties, between objects and the ways those objects are;
2. that that distinction is a very rough-and-ready one, and hard to make more precise.

In Descartes' day there was a sophisticated vocabulary for discussing such questions. Broadly speaking, the term used for what I have been calling a thing, such as an object like the LTP, was a 'Substance'. (So when you see the word 'substance' in the *Meditations*, don't think of stuffs or materials, like gold or steel or LSD; think of things, individuals or entities.) What I have called properties, aspects or ways that things are – like a thing's shape, for example – were standardly referred to as 'Modes'. Composite entities, like a coin collection, were often called 'Aggregates' or 'Entities by Aggregation'.

The way these terms were defined varied a great deal from author to author. By the use of them, they set out their differing accounts of what there is in the world – what exists and what doesn't, what is real, what is unreal, what is ultimate, what is dependent, and so on. They set out their different 'Ontologies', their accounts of What There Really Is.

More recently these questions have been much less discussed (though they have now come back into fashion), and the terminology has largely gone out of use. But we all have an ontology. It provides a kind of unspoken background to our lives, a mental map of the world. It serves as a basic framework, around which we construct our understanding of ourselves and the things around us. We don't talk about it, we don't think about it, but it is there. How would your life be different if you didn't have the concept of an object? If you didn't instinctively and unthinkingly differentiate between things and properties (as above)? Or what if you thought (as Spinoza did), that really there are no individual things in existence, and everything that exists is just an expression of the single Reality, which he called God or Nature? Or if you thought (as Berkeley did) that of course there are real individuals: but the only ones there are are individual minds, with their different experiences and intentions?

It seems to me that no-one can live without an ontology.[33] Because to live (for a person, at least) is to construct a view of the world, and an ontology is nothing but the basic structure of that view. So what is your ontology? What do you think, in the final analysis, the world really consists in?

Very few of us nowadays are Spinozists or Berkeleians. Most of us take for granted a common-sense ontology of physical objects, with their different properties, arranged in different ways – an ontology of Substances, Modes, and Aggregates. But that is a long way from the end of the story. As we saw above, objects like the LTP aren't in fact the basic elements of the world that we sometimes take them for because they are made up of material stuff which existed long before they did. Millions of years ago the LTP was sand and living things on the sea floor. Some time later it became rocks forming mountains. Then one day it was dug out and turned into blocks of stone, and those blocks were carved and assembled to produce the LTP as we know it. In a few years that same stuff could be rubble on an old battlefield; in a few thousand years perhaps just parts of a cloud of dust drifting through space.

So the LTP isn't, in the final analysis, really a *thing* at all. It's just a mode or an aggregate – a form that certain bits of matter are currently taking. And what is it a form, a mode or an aggregate *of*? What are the real things, the substances, that it is made up of?

Different people might give different answers, but most people, it seems to me, think that what really exists, in the final analysis, is an unthinkably large number of atoms and subatomic particles, out of which everything else is made up. Our understandings of those things tend to vary – some people think of them as like tiny, tiny billiard-balls, others as energy fields, or probability waves or whatever – but most people think that ultimately what there is in existence is huge, huge numbers of tiny, material bits. Those are the only 'substances' most people in our society allow.

If that is correct, then contemporary common-sense ontology is a kind of 'pluralism' (there exist a *plurality* of separate individuals) and a kind of 'atomism' (everything is made up of more-or-less interchangeable tiny bits. And the fact that what we call 'atoms' may themselves be divisible into smaller bits doesn't mean it isn't still an atomist ontology.)

Descartes' ontology is very similar in one way, but with two big differences.

1. His theory is like ours in that like us he holds that the world as we experience it – the world of planets and pea-pods and Portugal and pigs and everything else – is only a modal world, the appearance of a deeper level of reality. Like us also he thinks that to explain that familiar world we need to see how it derives from that deeper level, and that to do so we need to engage in the kind of practices that we now would call scientific investigations [3.1.11].

2. One important difference is that, as we saw above [3.2.8], he thinks that explanations of that kind can cover only part of reality, only part of what there is. His ontology includes, in addition to matter, *immaterial* substances – individual souls or minds – which are necessary to explain the things people do and which cannot themselves be explained through matter [3.2.6].

3. The second difference is very striking, but not in the end very significant. Whereas we tend to operate with a pluralist, atomist ontology, Descartes is a material *monist*: he thinks that ultimately the material world consists not of uncountably many individual units, but of a single continuum of stuff – one huge object, the parts of which are constantly in motion. And it is the way those individual parts or areas are arranged and operate on each other that explains everything that occurs in the physical world [3.2.4].[34]

Links

-   The question of the relation between ontology and language is raised in 3.2.7.
-   The issue of the ontology of wholes and parts (as in the LTP case above) comes up again in 3.3.6.
-   Berkeley's 'Idealist' ontology is sketched out in 3.5.4.

PART III: GOD

3.3.1 MEDITATION 3, SECTION 1. (34–6)

CLEAR AND DISTINCT IDEAS

Overview

So, I'm going to turn away from the world around me, and concentrate on what I now know myself to be – a thing which *thinks*, in these various different ways. Is there anything else I know (34–5)?

Well, if I'm certain I'm a thinking thing, doesn't that mean I know what it takes to be certain of something?

Why am I certain of the *Cogito*? Just because I can see clearly and distinctly that it *has* to be true. So can't I say in general that whenever I can clearly and distinctly see that something has to be true, it *is* true (35)?

'But hang on. I've often taken things for certain when they weren't – like the world around me.'

Yes; but what did I really perceive clearly? Just that I was having these experiences. And I was right about that. My mistake was in jumping to conclusions about the *causes* of those experiences (35).

What about simple *a priori* knowledge, like in arithmetic and geometry? Isn't that also certain? I only managed to cast doubt on it by thinking there might be an all-powerful God or something that made me such that I go wrong even about things I'm certain of. When I'm actually thinking these thoughts – like the *Cogito*, or 'If I exist, it will never be true that I never existed', or '$2+3=5$', or anything else which would be a contradiction if it were false – I am completely convinced by them, and there's only this theoretical, 'metaphysical' possibility that I could be mistaken. But I have to get rid of even that remote possibility of doubt, or I'll never be *completely* certain of anything (35–6).

Commentary

Three important steps in this little passage.

1. Clear and Distinct Ideas

The vital question at this point is how to move on from the discovery of the *Cogito*. The fact of having one thing she can't doubt isn't going to be of much use to The Thinker if that's all she can ever know, and this is the point at which she tries to build on it. The *Cogito*, she thinks, shows not only that I exist, but also and more importantly that *I can attain certainty*, I do have access to the truth. All I have to do, then, is to work out *why* I can't doubt the *Cogito*, and then I can use that as a tool to enable me to re-build the house of knowledge.

So what's the answer? What is the magic key that will take me from a knowledge of my own existence to a stable and secure knowledge of things in general? The answer tends to strike us as vague and disappointing: I can be certain of anything that I perceive 'Clearly and Distinctly'.

Does that strike you as a bit weak? Has the careful search for certainty and the refusal to accept anything that could be doubted just collapsed into the principle that you can believe anything you feel sure about?

Three things to say in Descartes' defence.

1. The *Problem of the Criterion* is the fact that it's impossible ever to provide a criterion of truth. Think about it. Imagine I discovered the Criterion of Truth – some property, call it C, such that any proposition which possesses Property C is guaranteed to be true. But how would I know I had the right criterion? Well, I would have to know that the proposition 'Any proposition which possesses Property C is true' is itself true. And how would I do that? I'd have to check whether it possessed Property C. But then, how would I know that the new proposition which stated that it *did* possess C, was also true? And so on, and so on, to infinity. The simple fact is, that unless you can *already* recognize when something is true, you will never be able to recognize what is the *true* criterion.[35]

    Descartes isn't trying to provide a criterion of truth, so if your disappointment with this step comes from the thought that he needs to provide one, then it is misplaced. His whole point is that we *do* have the ability to tell truth from false-hood, and his method works as a kind of therapy, which is designed to liberate that natural ability in people who he thinks have become confused by changing times and bad education. If we think through the Doubt, we will rediscover that natural, 'innate' ability, and will be able to use it to establish secure and lasting knowledge. What we need, therefore, is not a criterion, or a test for truth, but just a way of characterizing true thinking once we have identified an instance of it, as we have done here in the *Cogito*.[36]

2.   So what is it about the *Cogito* that makes me so sure it's true? It can't be that it possesses some special property, which I know to confer truth, because apart from the Problem of the Criterion, if it is to do its job as the turning-point of the Doubt the *Cogito* has to stand alone, to be something I can recognize as true without any evidence or backup of any kind. It has to be *self-evident* [3.2.1]. And how do I know it's self-evident? What test can I apply to tell me that it is? The question makes no sense. To say it's self-evident is to say that as soon as I understand it, I just *know* that it's true: I can see there is no alternative; for it to be false would be a contradiction, an absurdity, literally unthinkable.

In other words, if the *Cogito* is to be the self-evident turning-point Descartes wants it to be, then it will be impossible for him to give any further characterization of it; it will have to be something you just recognize, and all he can do is to point out what it feels like to encounter such a thing. And that is what he does. He says the only way you could go wrong about something like the *Cogito* would be if

(a)   you didn't understand what it was. Or

(b)   you did understand it, but you weren't thinking about it. (You learned about it years ago; you hear someone say it's not true, and it doesn't immediately strike you that they must be wrong.) Or

(c)   you do understand it, you are thinking about it, but you get confused. (You think of it as claiming that everything that exists thinks, instead of the other way round.)

But as long as you know what the *Cogito* is, and you think about it carefully, you *can't* go wrong about it, can you?

And that is all Descartes means by talking about Clear and Distinct Ideas. An idea is Clear if it is in your mind and you're thinking about it, and it's Distinct if you've not muddled it up with anything else {*Principles*, 1.45}.

3. So there is a reason why at this crucial turning-point, Descartes offers us not a criterion, not a test we can apply, but just a psychological characterization of what it is like to find something self-evident. Is it strong enough? Or is it just equivalent to saying anything you feel sure of is OK?

    This is the objection he brings against himself when he says, 'I previously accepted as wholly certain and evident many things which I afterwards realized were doubtful' (35). And his answer shows what Clear and Distinct Ideas are, and how he thinks they can work. This piece of paper in front of you seems perfectly obvious, beyond doubt. Do you perceive it Clearly and Distinctly? No. What you have is a very forceful ('clear') but unanalysed (not 'distinct') awareness of the sensations you are having, combined with a long-standing, habitual judgement that such sensations are caused by a piece of paper: not a Clear and Distinct Idea at all. Would it be a contradiction, would it be unthinkable, to say you're having this experience but the piece of paper doesn't exist? No. That's what the Dream Doubt proved [3.1.3].

2. *Building on the* Cogito

Descartes, then, says the *Cogito* is self-evident to anyone who knows what it is, and who is thinking clearly about it. And given the kind of project he's embarked on, it's hard to see that he could give a much better characterization of how we know it's true. The crucial question is, is he right that other propositions possess the same kind of self-evidence?

What do you think of the other examples he provides? Take '2 + 3 = 5'. Is that too something that you know must be true because you can perceive it Clearly and Distinctly?

It might seem not to be, because there are people who get it wrong. Not everyone can do even elementary mathematics, after all. And children make mistakes about sums as easy as this. But are they thinking Clearly and Distinctly about it? Surely, people who go wrong about it are people who don't know what it means, or aren't thinking about it or have muddled it up. Descartes says that anyone who understands it, and who is thinking carefully about it, will be convinced of it. Isn't that right? And of course, anyone who *isn't* capable of that level of understanding, or of knowing when they are thinking carefully, won't be in a position to follow The Thinker's train of thought in the first place. Again, what we have here is not an abstract criterion for people who know nothing, but a practical test for people who want to build on their innate ability to recognize truth.

Perhaps you will object that whereas the *Cogito* tells us a hard fact about what there is in the world – that I exist – a pure *a priori* truth like '2 + 3 = 5' tells us nothing about empirical matters, like whether as a matter of fact, people with two apples who get another three apples end up with five apples, or anything of the kind. The most it can do is to tell us about the *concepts* involved, and how they are connected [3.1.4].

But Descartes isn't claiming any more than that. He is very definitely *not* trying to say that by beginning with the *Cogito* we can build a complete knowledge of the world derived by deductive logic from *a priori* certainties. He is claiming two things:

1. That the things we can be most certain of are not, as it might appear, our judgements of the world around us, but these what you might call rational intuitions, simple *a priori* certainties like the examples he gives. Is that true? It seems to me that if you accept The Thinker's first move, that the whole world around us can be doubted, then it is hard to disagree.

2. That the ability to recognize these *a priori* certainties gives us the possibility of overcoming the deceptions of casual appearances, childhood opinions and bad education because it means we can *work out the implications* of our experiences [3.1.11]. So, for example (though for political reasons this is not an example Descartes himself could have given, even though he believed it), it looks and feels to us as if the Sun moves and the Earth stands still. That is a perfectly natural judgement for anyone to make, and it is one that was reinforced by tradition and authority at the time. But it is nonetheless a hasty, mistaken judgement, because it disregards the human element in our perceptions. It jumps from the undoubted fact that we have experiences of certain kinds – the path of the Sun across the heavens, the felt stability of the Earth – to conclusions about what is actually happening. But we can escape from those misleading appearances if we make careful observations, and work out their

implications by rational inferences – as men like Kepler, Galileo and Descartes were doing.

Or to put it another way, the Clear and Distinct perceptions of the unclouded intellect, which the example of the *Cogito* proves that we are capable of, enable us to overcome the deceptions of the senses through what we would now call scientific inquiry [3.4.5].

3. Doubting the indubitable

But there is an obvious question which has no doubt been troubling you while I have been trying to explain why I think Descartes' notion of Clear and Distinct Ideas is not the simple cop-out it may appear to be, which is that he seems illegitimately to have abandoned the doubts of Meditation 1 and to be treating all his rational intuitions as certain just because he found the *Cogito* to be something he couldn't doubt. But surely the Clear and Distinct Ideas of Meditation 3 are no more than the *a priori* truths he doubted in Meditation 1 by the Nature Argument – the thought that I might be made such that I go wrong even about things I can't doubt [3.1.5]. Worse still, if my account of the nature of Clear and Distinct Ideas is correct, then their special quality lies not in their logical form, or in some unique feature I have discovered them to possess in themselves, but just in the fact that if I think clearly about them I find them convincing. But surely that could be no more than a fact about *me* – that *I can't doubt them*; but that gives me no grounds at all for saying that they are actually *true*.

If you were thinking that, you were thinking exactly what Descartes thinks. That is precisely the point he makes in the section I have given as the last paragraph of my paraphrase above. Descartes' language here is sometimes misleading, but it is a tricky point to state clearly. Clear and Distinct Ideas are indubitable. It is a fact that I can't doubt them. But I *can* ask myself the question whether they are true – whether the fact that I can't doubt them is a good reason for saying that they are true, or is just a sad fact about me and my deceived and deceiving nature. But that means that in a sense they're not indubitable at all. I can't *feel any doubt or uncertainty* when I consider one; but I *can* ask whether that inability to doubt them is any guarantee of their truth.

And here we hit a big turning-point in the *Meditations*, and the very centre of Descartes' attempt to establish the possibility of genuine, *objective* knowledge. What Clear and Distinct Ideas give me is my understanding of truth and of certainty. They are the highest standard I can ever apply, they are my thought at its best, freed from prejudice, misleading appearances, bad education, carelessness and confusion. Does that mean they are true?

Descartes says that in itself it doesn't. He thinks that in order to show that my Clear and Distinct Ideas are true he has to show *more* than that they meet all my criteria for truth, that they pass all my tests. To prove that they are true he has to establish that, independently of what I might think and how my mind might work, these things are independently, *objectively*, true.

Is he right?

If he *is* right, then how can this ultimate doubt, which Descartes calls here a 'metaphysical' doubt and elsewhere a 'hyperbolical' or 'exaggerated' doubt {OR4, 226}, ever be answered? Since the doubt is about the adequacy of my standards and my procedures, then surely none of my tests will ever be able to remove it – that would be like trying to check whether what it says in your newspaper is true by going out and buying another copy.[37] Descartes, therefore, concludes that the only way he can answer the Hyperbolical Doubt, and can validate his thought as a whole, is by appeal to some independent, external standard of truth. But where can that standard be found? Other people can't provide it: they could provide at best a *shared* standard, but not an objective one; and until The Thinker has resolved the Doubt she has no reason even to believe that other people exist.

Descartes concludes that the only way we can resolve this deepest level of doubt is by appeal to God. If I can prove that God exists, then I might be able to prove that my best thinking is actually true; if I can't, I will never be able to escape from Scepticism.[38]

Are you happy with that move? And more importantly, can you believe in the possibility of objective knowledge without it?

Links

- Descartes' resolution of the Hyperbolical Doubt is in 3.4.1.
- The coherence of this kind of external guarantee of our thought is considered in 3.4.4.

3.3.2 MEDITATION 3, SECTION 2. (36–40)

THE NATURE OF IDEAS

Overview

I need to get clear about the different kinds of 'ideas' I have. We need to separate ideas in the strict sense – my *concepts* of things – from other kinds of thought that often go with them, such as emotions [I feel a certain way about something I have a concept of], decisions [I choose to do something about something I have a concept of] and judgements [I judge that something is true of something I have a concept of] (36–7). It's only the judgements that can be true or false – concepts, like emotions and decisions, can't be either (37).

Some of my concepts seem to be implanted from outside, some I just invent at will, and others arise from within my own mind (37–8).[39] I go wrong because I naturally assume[40] that the ones that come from outside accurately represent external causes (38–9). But the causes may not be external, and even if they are they may not be accurately represented (39). So I was quite right to doubt the external world (40).

Commentary

This section doesn't advance the story very far, but sets up some important preliminaries you need to be clear about.

How is The Thinker going to get out of her own head? She has established her own existence as a thinking thing, and with that the existence of her own thoughts. But how can she ever get from there to a knowledge of things outside her?

The answer is that she will look at those thoughts, and try to decide what they tell her about the world outside her own mind. In particular, in this crucial first step she will ask whether any of the concepts she finds in her mind is such that there has to be a real thing in the world which corresponds to it. And before she can do that, she needs to clear up what sort of ideas she has.

Basically she seems to me to make three points here.

1. *Ideas.* We need to separate out the concepts in my mind from the other kinds of thoughts I have. Descartes lists emotions, decisions and judgements, none of which could occur if

I didn't have the concept of the thing in question, that is, if I didn't know what it was.

He says here that strictly speaking only what I am calling concepts should be called ideas, but he doesn't keep to that usage, and he uses the word 'idea' for any kind of mental entity or event (any 'mode of thought'), so you need to be alert for different uses of the term.

What I am calling concepts he calls 'images' here, but that is misleading. We tend to use the word 'image' to mean something visual, like a mental picture. And Descartes himself often talks that way: he talks of images formed in the eye by light (*Optics*, 5.VI.114), and also of memories as traces left by images imprinted on the brain (Letter to Mesland 2/5/1644.IV.114), and he uses the word 'imagination' (sometimes 'fantasy') to mean thinking which involves the use of images in that sense. But here he has The Thinker use the word in a loose, non-technical sense to mean what we would naturally call my idea or concept of something – whatever it is in my mind that stands for, represents or refers to something outside me. (The fact that he doesn't mean an image as a picture is shown by the fact that he says we can have an image of God. God is immaterial, so we can't literally have a picture of God.)

2. *True Ideas*. Concepts, emotions and decisions can't be either true or false. He'll say later (43) that concepts can be 'materially false', by which he means you can have an idea of something which doesn't correspond to anything in the world, but here he is stressing that even when you go wrong – for example, if you think that Aristotle was a Belgian – it's not that there's something wrong with your concept of a Belgian Aristotle, any more than there's anything wrong with your concept of Sherlock Holmes. The concepts you have of those things are perfectly OK as long as we think of them just as concepts in your mind. Truth and falsity only come into the picture when you judge, when you decide, that the ideas in your mind accurately represent what exists in the world.[41]

3. *Innate Ideas*. The classification of ideas into innate, adventitious and invented comes up again in Meditation 6, where it

plays an important part in the proof of the existence of the material world [3.6.3]. Don't be misled by the term 'innate'. I said in 3.1.4 that when Descartes says an idea is innate (and he will later say that the concept of God is innate), he *doesn't* mean he is born thinking of it. (Even though many people including Locke have taken it that way.[42]) What he means is that the idea in question is *born within* him, that it is one which arises naturally in his mind (as opposed to either the idea of a tree, which I get from experience, or of a hippogriff, which I make by putting together bits of other ideas), and so must be in some way *built into my nature* (or innate) from the beginning.

Descartes will come to the conclusion that the idea of God is innate in us in just this sense. But it isn't the only one. Take the idea, for example, of a perfect circle. No experience you ever have can give you that idea because no circle you ever encounter is perfect. Yet we all have the idea, and it is the same in all of us. Descartes thinks that shows we don't just make it up: the ability to formulate such ideas is something built into the structure of the human mind, or the idea is 'innate' (OR5, 380–2). Similarly, he thinks the idea of *the self* is innate in the same way. After all, it is something we can't experience (it is the self which *has* experiences, so it can't be what is experienced), and yet, as the *Cogito* shows, we can be certain of its existence without any external evidence. That means the idea must come from within the mind itself, doesn't it?[43]

3.3.3 MEDITATION 3, SECTION 3. (40–2)

SUBSTANTIALITY AND THE CAUSES OF IDEAS
Overview
But everything I have said there concerns the *origin* of ideas. Let's look instead at their *content*. If we think of them just as ideas in my mind, they all seem to be on a par.[44] But in so far as they represent different kinds of things, they're very different, in that the things they represent can be more or less substantial (40).

Now, it's obvious that causes must be at least as substantial as their effects – otherwise something could come from nothing, or more from less.[45]

But the same applies to the *objects* of ideas: just as what is more substantial can't be caused by what is less substantial; so the *idea* of something more substantial can't be caused by anything less substantial than the thing it's an idea of. After all, ideas must in the end be caused by *things* (40–2).

Commentary

As I hope my paraphrase makes clear, the thought here is relatively straightforward. But the terminology makes it difficult to follow in the text.

The key terms are Formal Reality, and Objective Reality. But we need to start with Reality.

1. Degrees of reality

What can it mean to talk about things as having different levels of reality, to say that one thing can have more or less reality than another? Surely things are either real or they're not, and it makes no sense to talk of things which are a bit real, not very real, or realer than others. But actually Descartes isn't talking about reality at all {OR2, 165–6}.

The Latin word '*realitas*' comes from '*res*', which means a thing. Literally, therefore, it means 'thingliness', or as I have called it 'substantiality'. I've explained the notion of a substance in 3.2.9; here's a very brief summary.

Some knives are really sharp. But their sharpness, although it's real, isn't a real *thing*, in addition to the knife. Sharpness is just a property of some knives: take away the knife, and you take away the sharpness; take away the sharpness, and you still have the (blunt) knife. So the knife is a thing, a 'substance', while its sharpness isn't.

But the knife stands to the matter that makes it up rather as the sharpness stands to the knife itself. The matter that makes up the knife has existed from the creation of the universe, and will exist until its end. The knife is just a state that matter is in at the moment. Take away the matter, and you have no knife; take away the knife, and you have a disorganized mass of matter. So the knife is less of a thing, less of a substance, than is the matter it's made of. In Descartes' language (which here is the formal language of the 'Scholastic' tradition in which he was educated, and which he is trying to subvert), a knife has less 'reality' (is less of a thing, less of a substance) than the matter that makes it up, but more than its sharpness has.

2. Formal and Objective Reality

If that makes no sense, read 3.2.9 and hope it gets better. If it does make sense, the next step is pretty easy. All you have to do is to forget what you normally take the words 'formal' and 'objective' to mean.

When Descartes talks of an idea's *Formal* Reality, he only means its substantiality, in the sense I've just explained. In that respect, all my ideas are the same – they all have the same level of substantiality (the same Formal Reality), because they're all just ideas in my mind, states of my consciousness, 'modes' of my thought.[46] But ideas aren't just events in my head, they also *represent* things, or refer to things (they are 'intentional') – they have *objects*. And the things they represent, their objects, can be of many different kinds, some more substantial, and some less. *Descartes calls the level of substantiality of an idea's object the 'Objective Reality' of the idea* {OR1, 102–3}.

Get it? If a knife is more substantial than its sharpness, but less substantial than its matter, then it has more Formal Reality than the one, and less than the other. And that means the *idea* of a knife has less *Objective* Reality than the idea of its matter, but more than the idea of its sharpness, even though the *Formal* Reality of all three ideas is exactly the same.

3. The 'causal adequacy' principle

So far I have just been trying to explain Descartes' terminology. Here is the first actual point he makes: a thing can't be caused by something which is less substantial than itself.

Is that true?

It's a difficult question to answer, given that the idea of substantiality is not one we use very often. But does it sound plausible to you that shapes and colours might be put together in such a way as to create an object of some kind? Surely not. You can make an object out of other objects, but not out of mere *properties* of objects. Why not? Well, er . . . it's hard to say. But, however, you phrase it, in the end the answer is going to come down to the thought Descartes expresses by saying that a cause must have at least as much Formal Reality as its effect. For the same reason you couldn't put objects together to create new matter. (That one is less obvious, because we think of objects as being matter, and it doesn't sound crazy that you might put matter together in such a way as to generate new matter. It would violate the kind of Conservation Principle that is central to our and to Descartes' Physics, but it doesn't seem inconceivable. But what surely *is* crazy is the idea that you could create matter out of mere *states* of matter, which is what objects more properly are.)

The idea seems to me to be a plausible one – which just goes to prove the influence that our unacknowledged ontology has on our thinking [3.2.7; 3.2.9]. Descartes too takes it as something that's obvious, but he does add the argument that if a cause could be less substantial than its effect, then you would in effect be making something out of nothing: you would be making more out of less, so the extra would come out of nowhere.[47]

So far, then, so good. The next step is harder to swallow. Descartes extends the principle to ideas, and says that not only must an idea be caused by something at least as substantial as itself, it must also be caused by something at least as substantial as *the thing it's an idea of*. The basis of the thought, clearest in the last-but-one paragraph of this section, is that in order to explain, for example, my idea of a fish, we need to explain not only how I come to be able to have ideas (to explain the Formal Reality of my idea), but also how I come to be able to have an idea that is specifically *of a fish* (to explain its Objective Reality). Descartes' claim is that whatever explanation you offer will need to cite something that's at least as substantial as the fish itself.

Put in those general terms, the principle seems to me to be plausible. Descartes requires rather less than some contemporary philosophers, who hold that in order for any idea of mine to be the idea of a fish, it needs at some point, either directly or indirectly, to have been caused by an actual fish.[48] His thought is only that it must have been caused by something at least as substantial as a fish. But then, since I am myself at least as substantial as a fish, I could always have made that up for myself.

3.3.4 MEDITATION 3, SECTION 4. (42–5)

THE CAUSE OF MY IDEA OF GOD

Overview

So, the question is: are any of my ideas such that they must come from something outside me? If so, then I know I'm not the only thing that exists (42).

Apart from myself, the only kinds of things I have ideas of are God, objects, angels, animals and people. The last three are ideas I could invent by combining the first two (42–3).

My idea of objects, if we examine it carefully, is just the idea of an extended mass, plus those of substance, duration and number. All the other properties I think of them as having may be quite untrue of them (43–4).[49]

As such, there is nothing in my idea of an object that I couldn't have made up for myself: objects are no more substantial than I am, and the ideas of duration and number I can get from my own thoughts. Of course, I think of them as *bodily* substance, whereas I myself am only a thinking thing; but since bodily substances are no more substantial than thinking ones, there's no reason I couldn't have made that up (44–5).[50]

What about the idea of God? My concept of God is that of an infinite, all-wise, all-powerful creator, on which everything else depends. I couldn't create the idea of something like that, so God must exist to have caused that idea in me (45).

Commentary

Two points we have to think about here, the second obvious, but the first less so.

1. Learning from myself

Notice how Descartes asserts here that it makes perfect sense that he should have constructed the ideas of angels, animals and other people, as well as that of the material world, all by himself. Because they are individual things, individual substances, and he is also an individual substance, there is no impossibility in the suggestion that he might have invented them. Is that true?

Because The Thinker's attention, and ours, in this section is focussed on the idea of God, this question tends to get overlooked. But it is a big one.

Implicit in the whole structure of the *Meditations* is the belief that we know the world from the inside out. By performing the *Cogito* I am able, in addition to knowing that I exist, to produce an understanding, not of my particular character and history [3.2.2], but of what it is to be a thinking thing, an individual, a self. And on the basis of that understanding of my own being, Descartes says, I am able to construct an idea of other people (they are other individuals like me), and of material things (other individuals of a different kind). Animals and angels can then also be constructed, just as different points on the same scale.

For Descartes, of course, that structure makes perfect sense. He thinks each person is an atomic individual, a thinking substance with its own identity, created by God and assigned a special connection with an individual area of the material continuum [3.2.6]. Many people now are unconvinced by that view of the mind. But if we abandon it, should we also abandon the view of understanding that goes with it?

The following are the four questions to consider:

1. Can I really have an understanding of myself prior to and independently of an understanding of other people?

    Does a child as it grows develop a concept of itself and its wants and its needs, and then at some later stage discover that some of the things in its environment are of the same kind? Or do the two ideas develop in tandem? Does it only come to understand itself in relation to others?

    Does it even make sense to say I know myself just by being me? What does it mean to say I am *me* if it doesn't mean I am *not anybody else*? (Could you have a concept of *here* if you didn't also have a concept of *there*?)

2. If I *did* start from an understanding of my own case, would I ever be able to arrive at an understanding of someone else? If my only conception of what it is to think is that of what it is for *me* to think, my only conception of pain is that of *my* pain, and so on, how can I ever come to the idea of a pain or a thought which is *not* mine?

3. Similarly, could a grasp of my own self really be enough to ground an understanding of the external world? If my idea of being is that of being *me*, how could I think of external objects as having being in the *same* sense as I have it? Isn't it rather the case that I create an understanding of my

mentality, of my subjectivity, in contradistinction to the unfeeling objects around me, and that neither conception could possibly exist before the other?

4. If you *did* conclude that you couldn't really have a conception of yourself unless you also and simultaneously had a grasp of other people and of the unthinking world around you, would that mean you can't really doubt away everything outside your own mind, as The Thinker claims to in Meditation 1?

Big issues, which we can only hint at here. The point is that the way Descartes sets out to prove the existence of God reveals deep assumptions which we should be aware of. Those assumptions, because they concern the notions of the self and of the individual, have enormous psychological, social and political implications. Descartes' dualistic account of human beings makes sense of those assumptions. If we abandon his dualism, should we also abandon the notion of the individual that it gives rise to?[51]

2. The idea of the supernatural: Descartes' first proof of the existence of God

For The Thinker, everything turns on the existence of God. Unless we can know that God exists, we can't refute the Hyperbolical Doubt, there is nothing that can't be doubted, and we are back in the position we faced at the end of Meditation 1 [3.1.6; 3.3.1.3].[52] And yet this first proof of God's existence (we'll meet another in Meditation 5), when it comes, turns out to be surprisingly short. Once you have grasped the terminology in which it is expressed, the thought is actually fairly simple.

All The Thinker has to go on as a basis for the proof is her own existence and that of the ideas in her mind. The fact that she *has* ideas doesn't prove the existence of anything outside herself because they are just thoughts in her mind. The *content* of her ideas of other people, objects, animals and angels tells her nothing either because they are all things the ideas of which she could have invented for herself. But the concept of *God* is not; the only way she could ever come to have the idea of God is if God exists; God must exist as the only possible explanation of my having the idea of God.

It's probably true to say that not many people have ever been persuaded by this argument. But I think there's more to be said for it than might at first appear, and I'm going to do my best to show how it might be made to seem plausible. The following are the four points to consider in evaluating it.

1. First, let's be clear as to what it is we are trying to prove. The question of how sincere Descartes is in his attempts to prove God's existence and of exactly what kind of God he is trying to prove, are discussed in 3.3.9. But here is the basic point you need to bear in mind before you can decide whether or not Descartes' argument works.

   Although it is grammatically the same, the question of whether or not God exists is *not* a question of the same form as the question of whether there are mountains on the moon, or whether the Loch Ness Monster exists. The Loch Ness Monster, if it exists, is just *another* existent, another thing for us to add to our list of all the things that the universe contains. It may be exciting and interesting and strange, and different in all kinds of ways from other things we know already, but in the end it is just another being, in fact another form that matter takes.

   God is not of that kind. To say that God exists is not to say we need to add another existent to our list, but that we need a whole new list. God for Descartes and his contemporaries is by definition a being of a wholly different order, a *supernatural* being, and the question at issue between Descartes and an atheist is not that of whether or not there is another thing in existence, but of whether or not there is another *level* of existence – whether in order to make sense of everything that there is, we need to make reference to an infinite creative intelligence which is *above and beyond* it.

2. The thought that, if he exists, God is a being of a different order from the rest of existence helps to make sense of Descartes' use of the causal principle. I argued above that although it seems archaic, it *does* make sense to say that an effect must have at least as much reality as its cause, because it makes no sense for a new thing to be created by putting together properties or states of things [3.3.3]. With God the point is even clearer. God couldn't be created by other things

for two reasons. First, he is defined as the creator of everything; so the only thing that could create him would be something he created himself, which seems implausible. But second, the causal principle says in effect that supernatural beings can't be created by natural beings. If there is an infinite intelligence which underlies and explains the whole of existence, then it can't be produced by any of those things which are *in* existence, can it? Just as no combination of shapes and colours and so on could ever make up a *thing which has* such properties, no combination of natural objects could ever create a *super*natural or transcendent being.

3.   But Descartes' argument of course turns not on the cause of God, but on the cause of *my idea* of God. So the question is this: If all that existed were (as most of us nowadays tend to believe) just natural objects, how could we ever form the idea of a *super*natural being? Isn't it true that, just as no number of natural objects could be put together to form a non-natural object, so too the concept of a non-natural being can't be formed by just putting together the concepts of natural beings?

What do you think? The suggestion contrasts with Locke's suggestion later in the seventeenth century that the concept of God *can* be put together in just such a way – that by taking the good properties we have encountered in people and increasing them without limit, we can construct the idea of the infinitely perfect being.[53]

Your attitude to this will perhaps turn on your attitude to concepts like infinity. Can you really construct the idea of infinity by addition or multiplication, as Locke suggests? Or is the idea of infinity precisely that of a number which *surpasses* any number so constructed? According to Descartes, the idea of infinity, like that of a perfect circle [3.3.2], is 'innate' in us, in the sense that the human mind has the capacity to *go beyond* all the natural numbers to form the concept of an infinite number. And the idea of God, the infinite creative intelligence which explains the whole universe, must be innate in the same way. No experience we ever have can give it to us, so the idea of it must be built into the structure of the mind itself. And how can that have come about? Can any combination of natural forces result in our having the idea of what is beyond nature? Descartes thinks not.

4. One final thought to try and make this whole idea seem less strange. The way Descartes talks about innate ideas, and about God as leaving his mark on his creation (51), can make his whole picture seem like some kind of ancient fairy story. But it is not that. It may be a very different way of thinking from what we are used to, and it may be false, but it isn't crazy. As I've said, Descartes is *not* suggesting we are born thinking about God [3.3.2]. He is well aware of the importance of education in developing the understanding of God. It would be no kind of disproof of what he says to point out that there are people who do not seem to have formed the concept. His claim is that everyone *can* form the concept of a transcendent being, and that the idea cannot be either discovered from experience, or constructed out of other ideas that *have* been acquired that way. Our possession of it is therefore evidence – indeed he says a proof – that there is something beyond the natural world.

Links

- Descartes' understanding of God is considered in 3.3.9.
- The question of what kind of existence God has is discussed in 3.3.6.

3.3.5 MEDITATION 3, SECTION 5. (45–52)

OBJECTIONS AND REPLIES

Overview

The fact that I am myself a substance doesn't explain my having the idea of an *infinite* substance. And I can't *construct* the idea of the infinite by the negation of my own finitude. On the contrary, I can only understand that I am finite because I already possess the idea of what is *not* finite, that is, God. And the idea of God can't be a misleading appearance, like a secondary quality. Because it isn't at all confused, and it contains all of reality. It's true that I cannot *comprehend* God in my thought. But that doesn't mean I can't *understand* what God is (45–6).

But perhaps I don't understand myself well enough, and perhaps I *am* capable of producing this idea? Perhaps by gradually increasing my knowledge I could come to know everything. If I'm potentially infinite, perhaps I could do it? But no. The mere fact that I can improve shows I'm imperfect, whereas God is by definition perfect (46–7).

All that seems clear. Yet it's easy to lose sight of it when I'm distracted by the objects and concerns of daily life. So try this question: could *I* exist if God didn't? Then I would have to be created either by myself, by my parents, or by something else less perfect than I conceive of God as being (47–8).

It's much harder to create something than to improve something that already exists. So if I could make myself, I would have made myself perfect, which I'm not. And we can't avoid that by suggesting that I have always existed, and didn't need to be created. Because the existence of a thing at one moment doesn't entail its existence at the next moment; something has to *keep* it in existence from moment to moment. And that conservation is nothing less than a constant process of re-creation. So, am I constantly re-creating myself? No: if I were, then as a thinking thing I would be aware of it. And I'm not (48–9).

I can't have been caused by my parents or by some lesser thing than God, because of the argument above: my cause has given me the idea of God; so if that cause is not God, it must have got that idea from its own cause, and then the same question will arise again. Sooner or later we have to conclude that the cause is God (49–50).

It can't be the case that I was put together by a combination of different causes, or that my idea of God comes from several sources. Because the *unity* of God is a central part of the idea. And I can't have got the idea that all God's perfections are united separately from getting the ideas of those perfections themselves (50).

Even if my parents had brought me about, they certainly don't keep me in being. All they did was to bring about a certain arrangement in the matter which 'contains' my mind.

So, from the fact that I exist and have the idea of a most perfect being, it certainly follows that that most perfect being exists. My idea of God isn't a sensory one. And it isn't one I have made up. It is innate in me, as the idea of the self is innate in me. In other words, the mere fact of being conscious means two things: I am aware of myself as a limited individual, and I am aware of a greater, unlimited whole on which I depend. And the fact that I have that concept proves that that larger whole, which I call God, exists (50–2).

Commentary

This long and involved section is concerned with clarifying and defending the argument we've been working through, explaining why the idea of God is 'innate' and what that means, and refuting alternative suggestions as to where it could have come from. The Thinker runs the question of the cause of her idea of God together with that of her own cause, as she seeks to show why if God didn't exist it would be impossible for her to exist as she is, that is, with the ideas that she has. The reasoning is dense and hard to follow, and at times looks contrived and/or confused. The most important aspects I have incorporated into my commentary on earlier sections. Two additional things are worth pointing out here before we move on.

1. Conception vs. comprehension

Notice how Descartes deals with the difficult question of whether human beings can understand God – he says in one sense you can, and in another sense you can't. That can look like a bit of a cop-out, but it does make some sense.

Can you really form an idea of infinity? Well, you can and you can't. You can't have an idea of it in the way you can have an idea of a finite number: you can't *count* to infinity, the way you can (at least in theory) count to other numbers, and you can't have any other kind of distinctive experience of an infinite number of things, the way your experience of three things is different from your experience of two things. And there are lots of difficult questions about infinity. Is the infinite number of points in 1 cm smaller than the infinite number in 2 cm? Is the infinity which is the end point of the series of natural numbers the same as the infinity at which parallel lines meet? And so on. But you can understand what infinity means – you can define it precisely, you can specify how it differs from other related concepts, and you can perform various mathematical operations on it (46) {OR1, 112}.

Descartes thinks the same is true of God. You can't *envisage* God, in the sense of having an image of him or a distinctive experience of him. And there are many difficult questions about God which we will never be able to answer. So we cannot *comprehend* God in our thought (*comprehendere/comprendre*). But we can define God precisely, and differentiate the concept clearly from others, so we can *conceive* of God, or have a *conception* of him (*intelligere/concevoir*) (45–6) {OR5, A, Ixa.210}.

2. Creation and conservation

Have you ever asked yourself why things that exist *continue* to exist? It might seem a strange question.

If you build a sandcastle on the beach, it will continue to exist until the wind has blown it away, the sea has washed over it or some nasty child has jumped on it. But if nothing like that happens, why does it just *go on as before*? Is there some kind of principle of Existential Inertia, which says that nothing exists unless something brings it into existence, and things that do exist continue in existence until something destroys them?

With a sandcastle, the Cartesian Principle of Inertia will do the job [3.2.4]. The sandcastle is a particular local arrangement of matter. Bits of sand don't move around of their own accord; so once they are in a certain position they will continue in that position until something moves them. OK, but what about things that *aren't* just local arrangements of stuff? What about a particular *substance*, like matter or a mind, for Descartes, or an individual atom for us [3.2.9]? The Principle of Inertia will 'explain' why it doesn't move around, but not why it continues to exist from one moment to the next. To do that, we need the Principle of the Conservation of Energy: that the atom is a local concentration of energy, and while energy can be moved around and take different forms, it can't be destroyed.

But what kind of an explanation is that? *Why* can't it be destroyed? What prevents it? Do atoms have some kind of power or force that preserves them from moment to moment? Or is the Conservation of Energy just a way of saying that things *do* continue in existence, and we have no explanation for *why* they do?

Perhaps you think the question makes no sense. Descartes thinks it does, and he thinks it's just as crazy to say things *just do* continue to exist as it would be to say they *just do* come into existence in the first place. So if the *creation* of the world has to be explained by reference to God, so too does its *conservation*:

God brings a substance into existence at its beginning, but he also needs to perform the same kind of operation at every moment of its life if it is not to slip back again into nothingness (49).[54]

The idea seems strange. But perhaps equally strange is our lack of curiosity on the question. For Descartes, God's creation of the world was not an event at the start of time, but is a constant, ongoing *process*. God didn't merely create the world at some point in the past and let it run along in accordance with the laws he laid down; he is actively involved in *re*-creating it from one moment to the next. And to say that the world operates in accordance with certain laws is to say, not that *the world* behaves that way, but that *God himself*, in re-creating it, does so in accordance with certain rules he has laid down for his own creative activity [3.3.9].

***

Meditation 3 has advanced The Thinker's project significantly. By the end of it she has proved

1.   That the *Cogito* isn't the only thing she can't doubt: its indubitability is shared by all her Clear and Distinct Ideas.
2.   But she has also stepped back a little from the position reached at the end of Meditation 2, in that she now realizes that indubitability alone isn't enough to give her objective truth.
3.   She has, though, managed to show that if she thinks carefully about it, one of the things she can't doubt is that God exists: the mind's ability to construct the idea of a *super*natural being cannot be explained by any purely natural process.

Links

- Descartes' concept of God is examined in 3.3.9.
- The nature of the existence questions is discussed in 3.3.6.
- 3.3.8 looks at the role of proofs of God's existence in general.

3.3.6 DISCUSSION 12

THE BEING OF GOD: WHAT KIND OF EXISTENCE DOES GOD HAVE?

Does London exist? Sounds like a crazy question. No-one would suggest that there is a large hole in the south-east of England where London is usually thought to be. And very few people would subscribe to some sort of conspiracy theory which said that all the experiences people have had of London have somehow been faked, and all the images seen around the world are actually of somewhere else, or were mocked up in a studio. But still, it does make sense to ask whether we need the concept of London, and if so what kind of existence we should say London has.

After all, London (or any other big city you'd care to think of) isn't a separate place, over and above all its boroughs and districts and suburbs and satellites. Take away Wandsworth and Haringey, and Kensington and Chelsea and all the rest, and you're not left with the essential London – you're not left with anything at all.[55] London isn't an extra part, in addition to all those others; when we talk about London, we are talking about the whole lot. So, is it a mistake to say that London exists? Should we say that *strictly speaking* there is no such place, that *really* all that exists are the parts that make it up?

You might say that kind of thing if you were particularly concerned to stress that London isn't a separate place, but in most contexts it's surely not true. We have to say that London exists, for at least two reasons. First, many things are true of London that aren't true of any or even all of its parts. No London borough is capital of the UK or is the largest city in Europe; it isn't true that the aggregate of London boroughs staged the 1948 Olympics (many of them weren't involved at all), and there are people all over the world who have heard of London and have never heard of any of the parts that make it up. Second, we need to talk of the existence of London in order to express the complex interrelations and commonalities between its parts. London has a transport policy, weighting allowance, tourist board, sewerage system, accent and weather system, for example, none of which makes any sense if interpreted as belonging to the constituent parts. In general, people have a concept of London; and that concept plays an important part in the way they think, speak and act. So London exists as a hard fact of life.

Compare the case of London to that of the fictional city of Nodnol, which I have just invented and which is made up of half of Herefordshire, part of a small village in Japan, the Atlantic coast of Norway, and Guatemala. Nodnol is no less 'real' than

London, in the sense that it is just a name for a grouping of parts, not a separate thing in itself. But Nodnol doesn't exist, whereas London does, because the concept of Nodnol is not one that we need, whereas that of London is. If someone knew of the existence of the parts of London but didn't know they formed an individual city with its own identity, history, traditions and operation, they would be ignorant of an important fact – the fact that all those parts form a single city.

If that doesn't convince you, try another example. Imagine for a moment that every day of your life, everything you have ever done or has ever happened to you, has been recorded. (I don't know why.) And imagine further (if you can) that someone is interested enough to read and study all these observations, so that they come to know everything you have ever done. But imagine also that for some reason I can't think of the person who reads all these observations doesn't realize that they are all observations of the same person: she thinks she has read thousands of snapshots of different lives, not the life of one single individual. Question: Would there be something she didn't know? Yes, there would: she wouldn't know they were all stages in the same life. Would there be some *thing*, some further existent, which she didn't know of? It seems to me that there would. She would actually know all about you, but not that it was *you* she knew about. There would be no part of your life that she didn't know, but she wouldn't know that all those life-stages she was aware of were precisely that – stages in a single life. Therefore, like the person who knew the boroughs but didn't know London, she also would fail to *understand* the things she knew to exist, because she didn't understand a *further* thing that exists. But that further thing wouldn't be another entity on a par with those she knew already, but the organizing whole which explains them.

The point of these examples is just to show that questions of existence are more complex than they might at first appear. Sometimes it can be true to say that A exists, in addition to B, C and D, even though from a certain point of view it could be said that B, C and D are all there is. To say that London exists as well as all its parts, or that the person exists as well as all his/her time-segments, is to say that we need the concept of the underlying unity in order to understand the individual entities we are already familiar with. And it is a perfectly natural way of speaking or writing to express that fact by saying that London and the self exist in addition to all their parts. Could the question of the existence of God be in any way similar?

Links

- The notion of ontology is set out in 3.2.9.
- 3.3.7 looks at the nature of atheism, and its relation to theism.
- 3.3.8 asks what are the functions of proofs of God's existence, and what conclusions we should draw if they fail.

3.3.7 DISCUSSION 13

DO ATHEISTS BELIEVE IN GOD?

This probably sounds like a silly question. I ask it as a way of making two perhaps surprising points:

1. Most seventeenth-century atheists believed in God.
2. The beliefs of most twenty-first-century atheists are remarkably close to those of thinkers in the seventeenth century who believed in God.

1. Did seventeenth-century atheists believe in God?

The question of whether there existed any atheists in Europe in Descartes' time is not easy to answer.[56] But many people were accused of atheism, even though many of them certainly *did* believe in God. Here are some ways that could happen.

1. You could be suspected of atheism because you believed in God, but had beliefs about God which were different from those of the person who was attacking you. This was especially true if the attacker thought that your views were likely to harm the cause of religion, or to weaken belief in God – but since more-or-less any belief about God which as held to be false could also be held to be harmful to religion, more-or-less any unorthodox view could be called atheistic. Thus, for example, Descartes' friend Marin Mersenne (1588–1648) says he is combating atheism when he denounces Giordano Bruno (burned at the stake in 1599) as

'one of the wickedest men the earth has ever borne' because he didn't think God could have put the sun in a different place (xii; 230; 231–2). And later in the century, Spinoza – who held that everything in existence exists in and is conceived through God – was pretty universally denounced as an atheist.

2. You could be thought an atheist if you believed in God, but held unorthodox views about other things. Thus Galileo was called an atheist for asserting the motion of the Earth, and Descartes himself seems happy to use the term for those who deny the immateriality of the soul (To Plempius for Fromondus 3/10/1637; I.414).

3. You could be an atheist if you believed in God but you were thought to have pessimistic or despairing views about human beings and their possibilities. Thus sceptics and atheists were often bracketed together, partly because believing in the weakness of human knowledge might lead you to think we could have no knowledge of God, but also because Scepticism seemed to contradict the idea that we were made in the image of the all-knowing God.

4. Sometimes people were accused of atheism because although they believed in God, they held views which might be thought immoral, or to encourage immorality in others. (Since God is all-good, any attack on morality is an attack on God, and hence a form of atheism.)

As Stephen Gaukroger says in his biography of Descartes, 'the term "atheist" in the seventeenth century is a term of abuse rather than something with a precise meaning. In fact one precise meaning it does not seem to have had is a literal belief that there is no God' (196).

2. *Do contemporary atheists believe in God?*

Sometimes art does great disservice to philosophy. No educated and sophisticated thinker in seventeenth-century Europe thought that God was an old man in the sky. With or without a beard. No-one thought God had hands, or fingers. But of course, trying to represent visually an infinite, immaterial being is quite difficult; so very often in the history of art God has been represented as a heavenly father.

Of course, we can't generalize over all the different views of God that existed in Descartes' time, but here are some things that were generally held to be true.

1. God is the explanation of everything, the cause, the creator of the universe, the one reality behind all appearances. It makes no sense to ask what caused God: God is self-explanatory, and before God there was no time.
2. God's nature is eternal, timeless and unchanging.
3. God is infinite, all-powerful and all-pervading. It makes no sense to ask where God is: God is everywhere and nowhere.
4. God is the standard by which human beings can be measured. The concept of God is what grounds our understanding of what a human being is, and of what we can and should be.
5. God, the explanation of matter, is himself immaterial.
6. God is all-knowing.

Compare that list with what a representative contemporary atheist might believe.

1. The Big Bang is the explanation of everything, the cause of the universe. Everything that has happened since then is just a working-out of that one event. It makes no sense to ask what caused the Big Bang: time and causation began when the Big Bang happened.
2. The facts of nature which were laid down at or immediately after the Big Bang are timeless and unchanging.
3. Those facts constitute a single reality which is infinite, all-powerful and all-pervading. It makes no sense to ask where the laws of nature are: they are everywhere, and nowhere.
4. The facts of nature as revealed by science are what tell us what kind of thing the human organism is, its nature and its potentials.
5. Matter itself is a consequence of the basic facts of nature as laid down by the Big Bang. Those facts are not themselves material, but they are the explanation of matter.
6. The basic facts of nature constitute the ultimate answer to all questions, the final explanation of everything. A complete account of them would encapsulate the whole history of the universe.

I have of course deliberately selected the features of each story which have clear analogues in the other. Even so, the two lists seem to me strikingly similar. Is that because I have misrepresented them? Are there features you can think of which one side would accept and the other would reject?

What this discussion of Atheism I think shows is how complex a process is the evolution of thought. It is natural, but quite wrong, to think that the shift from Theism to Atheism that has occurred in Europe over the past few hundred years is simply the fact that people used to believe in God, and now they don't. To say that would be a bit like saying that the difference between a great novel and the three-line summary on the cover is that the summary is a lot shorter. In reality, Theism in the seventeenth century was not one belief, but many: a set of outlooks, attitudes or ways of seeing the world which were sometimes very different and sometimes surprisingly similar to ones we are familiar with. If we want to learn from their different views (as opposed to just dismissing them with the childish assumption that we know better), we need to look into their Theism, and to ask ourselves which parts of it we want to keep, which parts we want to reject, and why. When you look at Descartes' proofs of the existence of God, then, you should ask yourself, not 'Does the proof work?', but rather 'What, if anything, does the proof show?'

Links

- Descartes' conception of God is set out in 3.3.9.
- The nature of existence questions is considered in 3.3.6.
- The relation between a purely 'metaphysical' and more anthropomorphic God is discussed in 3.3.10.

3.3.8 DISCUSSION 14

PROOF, RATIONALITY AND
THE PRESUMPTION OF ATHEISM

Descartes advertises the *Meditations* as proving the existence of God (17), and sure enough, in Meditation 3 and again in Meditation 5 he sets out two different ways of showing that any rational person who considers the question without prejudice must agree that God exists. And according to me those proofs are not just an added extra that Descartes throws in to placate the authorities: the existence of God is crucial to the whole story of the *Meditations*. Without God, Descartes says we can never escape from the doubts of Meditation 1 (OR6, 428) [3.4.1].

Most people who read the *Meditations* think the proofs of God fail, and therefore that the whole project of re-founding knowledge on a firm basis falls apart. Hardly anyone has ever been convinced by the Meditation 3 proof [3.3.4], and most people nowadays think the Meditation 5 version was decisively refuted by Kant in the eighteenth century [3.5.5]. The question I want to ask here is this: if the proofs of God fail, what should a rational person conclude?

At first the answer may seem obvious. If Descartes needs to prove the existence of God, and if his proofs fail, then unless we have some better proof available, a rational person will not believe in God. The failure of the proofs wouldn't of course amount to a *dis*proof of God's existence, but it would mean that we haven't been given any good reason to believe that God exists, and if that is the case, then we can only conclude that a rational person will not believe in God. That's surely what it means to be rational, after all: a rational person only believes what she has good reason to believe, so in the absence of any successful argument for God, she will not believe in him.[57]

I have two points to make about that reaction.

1. Most people who have written about such questions in the past have taken the opposite view: that if reason fails to show God's existence, then, given that God exists, what it shows is the weakness of human reason, which is unable to encompass the great truths of life. Is that an irrational attitude?

2. If it is, then it seems that most of us are guilty of similar irrationality. As we shall see later, Descartes also offers a proof of the existence of the material world [3.6.3], which he had doubted away on Day 1 of the retreat [3.1.3]. Most commentators, both then and now, think that proof, too, fails to do the job. Most contemporary philosophers will also admit that they have no successful alternative to Descartes' proof, and therefore that the existence of the material world is something they cannot prove.

Now ask yourself this question. If you too came to that conclusion, that you could see no way of proving the existence of the material world, how would you react? Would you conclude that, as a rational person, you therefore have no alternative but to give up your belief in matter, and cease to think that human beings, whatever else they may be, are material organisms in a material universe? Or would you do what the great majority of contemporary philosophers do, and simply shrug your shoulders and say it just goes to show that not everything that's true can (at least at present) be proved?

I suspect most people will take the latter course. So my question becomes: how can it be rational not to believe in God because there is no proof that he exists, if it is also rational to believe in the existence of matter *even though* we have no proof of it?

What I think those points show is that rationality is not the simple matter we might think it is. If a rational person is someone who believes nothing without a sound argument, then I suspect there never has been and never will be a rational person in existence. Descartes and his contemporaries took as their bedrock, as their default position, a God-centred world; we tend to take as our bedrock the opposite. Which is the correct position? And how could you argue from one to the other?

When Descartes sets out to prove the existence of God, he is not assuming that his readers are atheists who will not believe in God unless his arguments are successful. Quite the opposite: what he is seeking to do by his proofs is to prove to the religious authorities of his day that the kind of rational inquiry on which he is engaged is not dangerous and subversive and atheistical, but actually confirms and strengthens the religious beliefs it was thought to challenge. His arguments are designed, in other words, not to prove God by reason, but to validate reason by showing that it can establish God. If you think his attempt fails, should we conclude that God doesn't exist, or that reason isn't up to the job?

Links

- Descartes' proof of the material world is examined in 3.6.3.
- The difference between theism and atheism is discussed in 3.3.7.

3.3.9 DISCUSSION 15

DOES DESCARTES BELIEVE IN GOD?
DOES HE *REALLY* BELIEVE IN GOD?
IS IT REALLY *GOD* THAT HE BELIEVES IN?

Descartes advertises the *Meditations* as proving the existence of God (17). Should we believe him? If so, can we assume that what he means when he says it is what *we* would mean if we used the same words?

1. Does Descartes believe in God?

Many people on reading the *Meditations* for the first time get the impression that the religious aspects of the book must be insincere. The search for knowledge seems compelling, they think, but the way he tries to answer his doubts by appeal to God seems so weak that it makes you wonder if he could possibly have taken it seriously.

And as you learn more, your doubts only increase. Descartes *never* simply writes down what he thinks, without having a very careful eye for what people will make of it, and whether it will get him into trouble.[58] The *Meditations* in particular is an especially duplicitous work, both in the way it presents itself as the earnest, wide-eyed investigations of a troubled Thinker, and at a deeper level in the way it tries to make itself acceptable to the Church authorities while actually seeking to undermine much of what they believe in [3.1.1]. So couldn't the part played by God in the story be just a gesture, an attempt to prove his orthodoxy by the use of arguments which he knows to be spurious? Doesn't the fact that it was only after he heard of the condemnation of Galileo that he started to write about God and the soul prove it's all just a cover, a pretence? There is so much in Descartes' writings that seems to us rational and modern: he argues that we should abandon tradition and authority and seek to establish a secure science of nature; and that science reveals the world as a single system governed by deterministic physical laws. Surely, the way he grafts the ideas of God and the soul on to that picture is a deliberate deception; or if not, then it is a testimony to the extent that he himself was unable completely to accept his own conclusions, and to throw off the prejudices and superstitions of his time.

I think that is a very natural way for anyone brought up in our world to understand the *Meditations*. But I think it is completely wrong, and reveals more about our own prejudices and lack of consistency than about those of Descartes.

To try and bring this out, let's assume for the moment that Descartes *does* believe in God, and ask what exactly it is that he believes in.

2. What kind of God does Descartes believe in?

At first sight, Descartes' God looks quite familiar and straight-forward. God is infinite and eternal, omniscient and omnipotent and all-good, the creator of the universe and of everything in it. The combination of God and mechanism is interesting. When God created the material continuum, he set its parts in motion, and produced a formless, incoherent Chaos of moving stuff (*Principles* 3.47). But that Chaos was anything but chaotic, because he also laid down the three laws which govern the ways in which that initial God-given motion is neither increased nor diminished, but passed around the different parts of the system by collisions. Over time the effect of those three laws was the development of the universe as we know it: relatively stable bodies of matter which we call stars and planets, and on earth a whole variety of living and non-living material objects [3.2.4].

Reading these passages makes the God of Descartes sound quite familiar. God is the Divine Engineer, who creates the mar-vellous mechanism of nature, lays down the laws of its operation, and sets it running. His involvement thereafter is primarily with human beings: he creates their individual thinking souls [3.2.6], hears their prayers, is concerned for their well-being, rewards them and punishes them, and so on. In the natural world, his only interventions are the occasional miracles he brings about – and those too are usually done for the benefit or enlightenment of people.[59]

On such a picture, if God did not exist, then the world would lose its point, its purpose and its explanation. All there would be is the endless sequence of physical processes. In such a world, human life would have no meaning; the only values would be those we create for ourselves; the only rewards and punishments would be human ones. In short, things would be pretty much the way most people in our society nowadays tend to think they are.

What that fact shows, I think, is that on this account God becomes a kind of optional extra in the system. The atheist and the theist are both agreed on the facts of nature; they disagree only about a further fact – the fact of whether or not, in addition to the world they are agreed on, there also exists a God.

There is much in Descartes' writing that permits this kind of view of his theology. The facts I mentioned above which could support an atheist interpretation of his work could also be used to show that the God he believes in is this kind of semi-detached creator figure who brings into being a world which he then merely superintends. And indeed, the very fact that Descartes tries to prove the existence of God surely supports this reading: if it were not possible to understand the world naturalistically, atheistically, if the facts of nature weren't ambiguous between a theistic and an atheistic interpretation, why would he need to *prove* that God exists? [For my answer to that question, see 3.3.8.]

But I think in reality Descartes would not recognize this external, creator God, and that the kind of God he is thinking of is much more intimately bound up with the world around us; so much so that, if we think of God the way Descartes and his contemporaries thought of him, his non-existence is quite literally unthinkable. That is why there weren't any real atheists in the seventeenth century [3.3.7]. And that is what his proofs are designed to show [3.5.5].

We have seen some of this alternative conception already. I argued in 3.3.4 that the question of the existence of God must be understood not as that of the existence or non-existence of another thing on a par with the things we already know, but as a question about the need to believe in a different order of being, or a completely different way of understanding the world. In 3.3.6 I suggest that the question of the existence of God is more akin to that of whether or not the whole exists in addition to its parts than it is to that of whether those parts are in any simple sense all there is. And in 3.3.5 I set out Descartes' belief that conservation and creation are the same: that the creation of the world is not an event at the beginning of time, but a constant, ongoing process. Putting those different points together now, we can perhaps begin to see a quite different account of the relation between God and the world from the one most people today are familiar with.

Descartes, of course, doesn't say much about God, in part because of his nervousness about having his whole project damned because of some theological dispute, in part also simply because his great discoveries were in the fields of Physics and Metaphysics, and he had nothing much to say about religion that wouldn't be already accepted by most of his contemporaries; so it is not surprising that he doesn't set out his theology in much detail.[60] One crucial passage where he does talk about the concept of God is *Principles* 1.51–2, where he explains that God is the only true substance, because God is the only thing that exists in such a way as not to depend on anything else for its existence. What does that mean?

I have explained the notion of a substance in 3.2.9. The basic idea is that a substance is a thing, an independent existent, as opposed, for example, to properties or actions, neither of which can exist unless there exist real *things* – substances – to bear those properties, or perform those actions. I said in 3.2.4 that whereas we tend to think that the real substances of the world – the ultimate constituents of nature – are atoms or other subatomic particles, Descartes thinks the whole of matter is a single substance, as is every individual mind. Given that background, what does it mean when Descartes says that God is the only true substance, and that minds and matter are substances in a different sense because while everything else in nature depends on them, they depend only on God for their existence?

Most people take the passage in a purely causal sense: matter and minds depend on God because he produced them; without God they wouldn't exist. That is of course true; but I think it tells only part of the story. I think we need to understand that created substances are dependent on God not merely causally but *ontologically*: that God is the single underlying reality which they express.

On this reading the relation between God and the created world is to be understood as analogous to that between a mind and its thoughts, or between matter and particular material things – or in contemporary terms between the atoms or subatomic particles of which the world ultimately consists, and the world as we experience it. God, in other words, is not the originating maker of the world, but the in-dwelling reality of it; the universe is not his creation or his product, but his ongoing *activity*.

If God did not exist, therefore, the world would not remain as a pointless mechanical system; it would be like an action without an agent, or a property without a bearer: it would be non-existent, an obvious impossibility.

This is the picture we get when Descartes talks of creation as not an event, but an ongoing process {OR5, 369–70} – the continual 'emanation' of the world from God. Even the deterministic mechanical laws which seemed to support the idea of a creator God who set up the system and left it to run, turn out to have a different reading. If the world is God's ongoing activity, if the universe is constantly re-created from moment to moment, then those laws are descriptive, not of the nature of created matter, but of God's creative behaviour. And that is exactly what Descartes says of them: the laws of inertia, straight-line motion and conservation are descriptions of the fact that God never acts without a reason, and that the noise and confusion we see in the world around us is only a misleading appearance of the constancy and order of God's actions {*Principles*, 2.36–42} [3.2.4].

What all this means is that divisions which we take for granted simply cannot be made out in Descartes' system. For us, science, religion and morality are separate fields, largely independent of each other. An atheist scientist, after all, can have a perfect knowledge of nature, and no hint of religion – in fact many of us think that science and religion are necessarily opposed, and that the more we know of the one the less we can have of the other. And morality and science are generally taken to interact only negatively, in the sense that moral concerns often *get in the way* of scientific investigation (think of all the arguments about cloning and embryo research). Morality and religion are often linked, it is true; but most of us now think it is possible to be a perfectly good person and also an atheist. For Descartes, those divisions would all seem artificial and quite absurd. To know the world as it is, through science, *is the same thing* as knowing God's ongoing creative activity; to engage in science is to seek to leave behind the promptings of the flesh, and to know the world non-sensorily, as God himself knows it; and to know the nature of human beings and their relation to God and to the world is to know our moral obligations.

The story I am trying to tell, then, is that we cannot begin to evaluate the argument for the existence of God in this section until we have understood

1. How it is meant to work [3.3.4].
2. What kind of thing Descartes understands God to be (which may not be at all what we first think of when we see the word) [3.3.9].
3. What kind of existence God is to be thought of as having [3.3.6].
4. What exactly the proofs are designed to do [3.3.8].

3.3.10 DISCUSSION 16

GOD AND GOODNESS: ANTHROPOMORPHISM AND RELIGIOUS LANGUAGE

Anthropomorphism means representing – and sometimes mis-representing – non-human things in human terms. So talking of an angry spot on someone's nose, the cruel sea or mother Earth, are all examples of anthropomorphism. In relation to God, the word is used for the mistake of attributing human qualities to God, or thinking that words which work perfectly well when applied to people can work in the same sense when applied to God. But to take some obvious examples, God (who is every-where and/or nowhere) can't be *in* heaven in the sense in which I can be in a bus station; God (who doesn't have vocal chords) didn't *say* 'Let there be light!' in the sense in which I might say 'Can I have a pickled egg, please?', and God, despite being all-good, doesn't give all his money to charity. The Problem of Religious Language is the problem of trying to avoid describing God in human terms while still describing him (her? it?) in terms that humans can understand.

It seems to me that because in contemporary Western culture God plays a much less central part than he did in that of Descartes' day, the problem of anthropomorphism affects us in a particular way. As many fewer people are now schooled in the language of religion, we tend not to appreciate the special sense (or is it *non*sense?) that has to be given to terms referring to God, and so we are in danger of trivializing the concept when we encounter it. For most people, when they see Descartes' attempts to prove the existence of God, his proofs seem to be trivial and obvious failures. Is that because he didn't actually believe in God, and was presenting specious arguments just to please the authorities [3.3.9]? Is it because he was actually rather stupid, and didn't know a good argument from a bad one? Or because the minds of people in those days were so clouded by ignorance and superstition that even the cleverest among them couldn't think clearly about God the way we can now? Perhaps. But perhaps also it is not his failure, but ours: that we are reading into his text too modern, too simple, too anthropomorphic a conception of God, and so accusing Descartes of failing at something he never actually tried to do.

I explained something of what I think is Descartes' less anthropomorphic, more metaphysical conception of God in 3.3.9, and in 3.3.7 I suggested that many contemporary atheists would in fact agree with a great deal of what Descartes means when he says that God exists. In 3.3.4 I tried to show that the 'proof' of 'God' in Meditation 3 does have some force for showing that the idea of a supernatural being couldn't be acquired naturally, but must be what he calls 'innate' in us [3.3.2]. The question I now want to ask is this: *if* we were to allow that Descartes has given us some reason to believe in a single, infinite substance – in other words to believe that the natural world is not all that exists, and there must also be a single, infinite creative power of some kind which does not itself exist in time and space, but which explains all the things that do so exist – is there any reason at all why we should refer to that infinite substance as *God*?

The question is complex, and we can only scratch the surface of it here. What I will do is take three qualities that have often been attributed to God, and see in what sense, if any, they might be applied to the more metaphysical conception of God that I am suggesting Descartes held.

God is often thought of as being *omnipotent* or all-powerful. Is the single substance which underlies all of existence omnipotent? Well, not if you think of omnipotence anthropomorphically, as being able to do whatever you feel like. An infinite substance doesn't feel like anything; it doesn't have whims or fancies or desires, it just *is*. But in so far as it is the ultimate explanation for everything that happens, you could say it does everything, and in that sense is all-powerful. And if you think that the underlying substance of the world is the reason why some things are possible and some are not, then everything that happens is everything that *could* happen – so the infinite substance does everything that's possible, or it is omnipotent.[61]

What about *omniscience*, or all-knowingness? Is the infinite substance omniscient? Not if you think of that as meaning it knows what's for tea and could tell you where you'd left your keys and what that funny noise is that you sometimes hear in the night. But if it is the explanation for everything, the source of all being, then it is in a sense the ultimate truth, and you might come to think of it as containing within itself all that can be known, and so in a sense as omniscient.

You're probably thinking that this is a kind of cheat, and that all I'm doing is redefining religious terms so as to show how they might perhaps be applied to something other than God. I think I'm doing more than that: that I'm explaining something of what these words used to mean before we lost touch with the idea of God and came to think of him as something like a superhuman old man who lives in the sky.

The real test for this kind of approach is perhaps the idea of God's *omnibenevolence*, or goodness. Surely only something like a human being can possibly be good – at least in the moral sense in which God is said to be good. Is it possible to think of God's goodness in a non-anthropomorphic way?

Well, there are ways in which it can be done. Start from the idea of the unreality of evil. Human evil, or moral failings, according to this way of thinking, are literally *failings* – they are failures, weaknesses, inadequacies. We are angry because we are scared, because we *lack* the courage to accept the situation. We are cruel because we are hurt, and try to revenge ourselves, or because we are trying to make up for our *inadequacies* by enjoying our power over others. We do bad things because we are *overcome* by greed, or envy or lust because of the *weakness* of our will, or because we *fail* to understand the situation appropriately. There is a very strong current in our moral language, in other words, which sees immorality in purely *negative* terms. But if God is the single substance which underlies all appearances, from which the created universe flows forth or 'emanates' at every moment, as the light flows out from the sun, then God is all reality, and cannot lack anything. It seems to follow that God is all-good. And when we say that, what we mean is not that God never loses his temper or acts out of spite, but rather that people who do those things are demonstrating their weakness and finitude, in contrast to the boundless wholeness and perfection of God.[62]

***

I am not in this section attempting to convert atheists to religion. (Since I am an atheist myself, that wouldn't make much sense.) Rather, I am trying to persuade you of two things:

1. That sophisticated seventeenth-century theists had a rich and complex set of interconnected beliefs which they expressed by the claim 'God exists', and that we should not represent them as believing simply what a contemporary atheist would deny.
2. That, therefore, we should not take Descartes' attempts to prove the existence of God as attempts to prove the existence of something out of a Sunday-school picture book.

Links

- The question of God's goodness comes up in 3.4.1 and 3.6.3.

PART IV: THE POSSIBILITY OF KNOWLEDGE

3.4.1 MEDITATION 4, SECTION 1. (52–4)

THE DISPROOF OF SCEPTICISM
Overview
So I now realize that, contrary to what I used to think, I don't know the world around me very well; I know my own mind much better, and God best of all. And now that I've got that sorted out, I think I can see a way forward (52–3).

God by definition couldn't deceive me. So he couldn't have given me a power of judgement which goes wrong even when I use it correctly (53–4).

Commentary
It's easy to overlook this little passage. Yet it is a crucial turning-point, where the deepest of the doubts The Thinker has raised is finally put to rest. If you can accept the argument that Descartes offers here, there will still be a lot to do (most obviously, we will still have no reason to believe in the existence of the physical world [3.5.1]), but you will have to accept that the most radical Sceptical position has been disproved, and that we *can* have objective knowledge. The *Cogito* showed there were some things we can't doubt [3.2.1]; we generalized that to say we can't doubt anything we can perceive Clearly and Distinctly [3.3.1]; but that only opened the door to the deepest, 'hyperbolical' doubt that perhaps our Clear and Distinct Ideas are false *even though* we are unable to doubt them. That would mean we can have no genuine grasp of how things are in themselves, and that all our claims to knowledge are in reality founded on nothing more secure than a kind of unprovable instinct [3.3.1].

So a lot rides on this little argument. Does it work? Two questions you need to ask yourself: is The Thinker justified in saying that an all-good God wouldn't deceive her? And (if we assume for the moment that she has proved the existence of God), is she entitled to say that God is all-good?

The first question is the easier. *If* you think that God made you, and *if* you think God is all-good, can you also think he has made you in such a way that no matter how hard you try, you can never discover the truth? That he has given you a nature such that you will of necessity always be deceived? Providing we accept the distinction between how things are for people and how things are in themselves [3.3.1], then you can perhaps see why Descartes says that it *couldn't* be the case that God made the human condition as completely hopeless as the Hyperbolical Doubt would have us believe {*Principles*, 1.30}.

But what about the other step? *If* you accept that the Meditation 3 proof of God's existence works, and that The Thinker is justified in holding that God exists, do you think she is *also* justified in holding that God is all-good?

Your answer to this will involve the whole question of the nature of God, and the nature of goodness. I suggested in Part 3 that Descartes' proof *does* have some force if taken as an attempt to show there must be a single reality which explains all the phenomena of nature [3.3.4]. And in 3.3.10 I tried to explain the relation which the seventeenth century saw between reality and goodness: that since evil is only the absence of good, it follows that the reality of everything cannot be evil, but must be all-good. The question you now have to ask is whether that 'metaphysical' conception of goodness is strong enough to rule out the pessimistic vision of a human race forever cut off from reality. Does this argument only go through on a more anthropomorphic reading of God's goodness?

3.4.2 MEDITATION 4, SECTION 2. (54–62)

MISTAKES, AND HOW TO AVOID THEM
Overview

So if God guarantees my thought, how can I ever make mistakes? Error isn't something real, it's the lack of something; but why has God made me lacking or defective in this way (54)?

Mistakes come from a combination of Intellect and Will: my Intellect presents me with an idea, and my Will decides whether it is true or false. So the Intellect doesn't cause my mistakes – it just presents ideas for me to consider. I can't understand everything, but the things I do understand, I understand correctly. My Will is the opposite: I can will anything at all, but because I am free, I can will wrongly. Mistakes come from the fact that I use my error-prone, but unrestricted, Will to believe things that lie outside the range of my clear but restricted Intellect (56–9).

So, I now see that if I can withhold judgement from things that I don't perceive Clearly and Distinctly, I need never go wrong (59–62).

Commentary

I have left out of my sketch of the argument interesting material on Final Causes,[63] and on Freedom. For the purposes of making sense of the story, there are two points to look at here.

1. Error and the Will

Have you ever asked yourself what the difference is between believing something – thinking some proposition is true – and merely understanding it? For example, you know (roughly) who Julius Caesar was, and you know what camel-riding is; so you can understand the proposition 'Julius Caesar once rode a camel', even though you probably (like me) have no idea whether or not it's true. If you then find out somehow that he actually *did* ride a camel one day, what changes? It's the same proposition that is in your mind, but now you're thinking it in a different way – you're affirming it, thinking it's true, applying it to the world, agreeing with it, whereas before you were just contemplating it, wondering about it, considering it as a possibility.

Descartes describes that difference in terms of two kinds of thought of which the mind is capable – Understanding (which he also calls the Intellect, a kind of Perceiving) and Will. You don't understand the proposition any better after you find out it's true than you did before; what happens is that in the light of the evidence you have discovered, you *give your assent* to it, or *affirm* it. And that is a matter of judgement, decision, choice or Will.

Does that seem plausible as a piece of psychology?

It is open to the objection that we don't always have a *choice* over what we believe. If you go for a walk and the clouds roll in and the thunder starts and you get soaked, it seems crazy to say you *choose* to believe it's raining, as if there were some alternative. But then, it's often true that we can't help but do something (jump out of the way of a charging rhino, eat too many vol-au-vents, remember being humiliated), but it's still something we do deliberately, something we *choose* to do.[64] And in so far as believing involves a judgement, it does seem to involve a decision, so it doesn't seem unreasonable to describe an act of judgement as some kind of *action*, an act of Will.

But whether it's true or not, you have to admire the way the theory fits into Descartes' story. Because the Will is involved, God is no more responsible for my false beliefs than he is for my immoral actions: God gives me everything I need for truth and justice – an Understanding which is capable of detecting the truth, and a free Will – and what I do with those tools is up to me.[65] That is why he stresses that each of the two 'faculties' is perfect in its own way: the Intellect is perfect in its nature, but limited in its range – I *am* capable of understanding things correctly (as The Thinker discovered in the last section, Clear and Distinct Ideas are objectively true), but I can't understand everything because we are only finite beings. The Will by contrast is the opposite: it is unlimited in its scope, but flawed in its nature: there is nothing I can't will (want, opt for), but because I am human I often choose wrongly. So mistakes occur when I give my assent to things I haven't Clearly and Distinctly understood.

What we have, then, is a theory which at least at first sight seems to fit the facts of experience, fits perfectly into Descartes' account of the mind and of the nature and possibility of knowledge, and harmonizes exactly with traditional Christian doctrine. I argued in 3.3.9 that for Descartes science, religion and morality are not, as they are for us, separate areas of inquiry but a single field, and here we see the same story: making rational, scientific judgements is not the right thing to do just because it gets to the truth, but also because in doing so I am simultaneously worshipping God, by knowing his creation better, and recapitulating in my own small way his purely intellectual grasp of it; and I am doing my moral duty by using my Free Will to rise above the distractions of the senses.

2. 'It is quite impossible for me to go wrong'

At the end of Day 4, then, Descartes has shown how he thinks we can disprove Scepticism, and has also explained how mistakes can nevertheless arise. But the position The Thinker ends up in seems way too strong. She says that if she remembers to confine her assent to only those things that she understands

Clearly and Distinctly, 'it is quite impossible for me to go wrong' (*non potest ut errem*/*il ne se peut faire que je me trompe* – 62).

But that seems crazy. Does Descartes really think that he will never make another mistake in his life? That if we follow his reasoning we too will be immune from error for ever more?

I don't think we need to attribute such a strange view to him. There are two alternatives we might take. One is to say that what he means is only that it will never be *necessary* for us to go wrong. Just as it is never necessary for us to sin, in that we always have a choice, so it is never necessary for us to make a mistake, because as we have just seen error, like sin, comes from our making the wrong choices. On this reading, a life without error is something we can aspire to, even if in practice we can never manage it.

But even that is surely too strong. While it may (perhaps) be conceivable that a person might never commit a sin – never get angry, never have lustful thoughts, never covet her neighbour's donkey or whatever – it is surely not even conceivable that a person might never make a mistake. That would mean never thinking the round tower in the distance was square, never falling over because you think there is another step on the stairs, never thinking someone had said 'grey tape' when they had said 'great ape', and so on. I can perhaps imagine a person who just *got lucky* in that way – just as it is conceivable that monkeys playing with typewriters would in an infinite length of time eventually type out the works of Shakespeare, so it is conceivable that one day there might be born a person who just *guessed right* every time she made a judgement – but the idea that we might discover a method of ensuring such a result seems at best implausible.

So why does Descartes say it? The first point is that we need to remember the way the whole project was set up at the beginning. Descartes is trying to 'establish [something] in the sciences that [is] stable and likely to last' (17). That means he is not primarily concerned with finding out the price of fish, or the time of the next bus or whether there's another step on the stairs [3.1.2]. So when he says here that we need never go astray, he doesn't mean we can avoid making mistakes about things like that. After all, none of those is something we can perceive Clearly and Distinctly. I don't perceive Clearly and Distinctly that the sun is shining, no matter how obvious it is – I just *see* it, and sensory knowledge isn't Clear and Distinct. I don't perceive Clearly and Distinctly what I did yesterday, even when I have no doubt about it at all – it's just a memory impression. I don't perceive Clearly and Distinctly the date of the Battle of Hastings – it's just something I've been taught, and remember. So what *do* I perceive Clearly and Distinctly, and what are the things I can never go wrong about?

The answer is the unchanging facts of nature that I have established by rational inquiry, or as we would say proved scientifically – such facts as the laws of nature, and also basic metaphysical truths about the nature of God, people and the universe. If you have collected the information about such things, done the necessary experiments and *thought through the implications* of what you have observed, then the judgement you make is not sensory, but rational. It is a judgement of *logic*. And judgements of logic are Clear and Distinct Ideas [3.3.1; 3.4.5].

What Descartes is saying, then, is not that if we read the *Meditations* we will become omniscient or infallible, but that if we apply scientific methods, we can come to have objective knowledge of the nature of the world around us. (And of course, when we have acquired such knowledge, we will find that things are just as Descartes said they are.) He will later go on to explain how we can also have reliable (although not infallible) knowledge of day-to-day matters [3.6.4].

Is that still too strong? Can we really have objective knowledge in science [3.4.5]?

Links

- Descartes' view of scientific knowledge is discussed in 3.4.5.
- His account of day-to-day knowledge comes in 3.6.4.

***

Meditation 4 seems rather undramatic, after the Doubt of Meditation 1, the *Cogito* in Meditation 2 and the Proof of God in Meditation 3. But don't let that mislead you into thinking nothing happens in it. By the end of it, The Thinker has

1. Finally disproved Scepticism, by rebutting the Hyperbolical Doubt that emerged in Meditation 3, and
2. Shown how objective knowledge is possible if, and only if, we follow the way of reason, or as we would say, the way of science.

3.4.3 DISCUSSION 17

'THE CARTESIAN CIRCLE'

Here's a possible summary of Descartes' disproof of Scepticism.

In Meditation 3 he tries to prove that God exists. He generalizes from the case of the *Cogito* to say that things I can perceive Clearly and Distinctly I can't doubt, and then tries to show that I can Clearly and Distinctly perceive that unless God really existed I couldn't have the idea of God that I do have. Then in Meditation 4 he argues that the fact that God exists and is good proves that my Clear and Distinct Ideas are true.

Does that strike you as a problem? Does it strike you as in any way a *circular* argument?

Many people have thought so. Ever since the book was published, commentators such as Antoine Arnauld (OR4, 214) have objected that the argument is blatantly circular. How do we know that God exists? Because we perceive it Clearly and Distinctly. And how do we know that Clear and Distinct Ideas are true? Because God exists and is no deceiver. But surely, if we don't know that Clear and Distinct Ideas are true, we don't know that God exists; and if we don't know that God exists, we don't know that Clear and Distinct Ideas are true.

The objection has raised a great deal of discussion over the years since 1641. To my mind, though, much of that has been work wasted, because I think the objection shows a failure to grasp the structure of the *Meditations* and the subtlety of Descartes' argument. But that doesn't mean there isn't still a problem.

As I tried to bring out in the Commentary, it seems to me that The Thinker is not assuming that Clear and Distinct ideas are true, but trying to show that they *must* be true because they are indubitable. In other words, her train of thought is not

Argument A

1. I have a Clear and Distinct Idea that God exists and is no deceiver
2. so it's true that God exists and is no deceiver
3. so Clear and Distinct Ideas are true

— which would be circular, but more like

Argument B

1. I can't doubt my Clear and Distinct Ideas
2. I have a Clear and Distinct Idea that God exists and is no deceiver
3. So I can't doubt that God exists and is no deceiver
4. So what I can't doubt must be objectively true.

The problem with Argument A is that you can't get from 1 to 2 if you haven't already established 3 – you don't know that God really is no deceiver unless you know your Clear and Distinct Ideas are true. But you can only get to 3 from 1 and 2, so you are arguing in a circle.

Argument B doesn't have that problem. Steps 1–3 don't assume Clear and Distinct Ideas are true, so there is no circularity.

Of course, that doesn't mean the argument works, only that if it doesn't work, that isn't because it's that kind of simple circle. You may think the argument doesn't work because a good God might still deceive us, or because Descartes hasn't proved that God exists and is good [3.4.1]. But even if you think he can overcome those problems, there is a further, structural question to be asked. In Argument B, does 4 really follow from 1, 2 and 3?

Perhaps 1, 2 and 3 will only give you, not 4, but

5. I can't doubt that my Clear and Distinct Ideas are true.

See what I mean? It may be that we have avoided the Circle only by an unjustified leap, from what I can't doubt, to what is actually true. But that is exactly the gap that this argument was meant to bridge, isn't it?[66]

What we have here, I think, is a particular instance of a general problem: the Problem of Justification. Descartes is trying to reply to the doubt originally created by the Nature Argument [3.1.5; 3.3.1] by showing that no gap can open up between what the best human knowledge says is true, and what really is true, or between how things are for us, and how things really are in themselves. The problem is that since Descartes is a human being writing for other human beings, the only tools at his disposal are the tools of human reasoning – the tools of argument and evidence and persuasion. Unfortunately it is precisely the reliability of those processes that is at issue. He tries to solve that problem by appealing to a non-human standpoint, the objective perspective of God. But while it may be true that *God* could solve the problem of the justification of human knowledge, I don't think The Thinker's (or anyone else's) *knowledge* of God can do it without at some point running into some version of the Cartesian Circle. Which is why I think the kind of certainty that Descartes offers us, and that many people think is necessary if we are to avoid Sceptical despair, can never be attained.

If that doesn't make sense, the argument is set out in more detail in 3.4.4.

Links

- For Clear and Distinct Ideas, see 3.3.1.
- The Hyperbolical Doubt and Descartes' way of answering it are covered in 3.3.1 and 3.4.1.
- The anti-objectivist argument is explained in 3.4.4.

3.4.4 DISCUSSION 18

SCEPTICISM, OBJECTIVISM AND CERTAINTY

Descartes tries to solve the Problem of Objectivity by proving that what he calls our Clear and Distinct Ideas are not only indubitable, but absolutely certain and objectively true [3.3.1]. The fact that views differ shouldn't make us despair of ever finding a final answer [Chapter 2; 3.1.2]. If we escape from the misleading appearances of the senses, we can find stable and lasting knowledge which we can all agree on, by means of the kind of rational interrogation of experience that we nowadays call science [3.4.5]. And those scientific judgements are not just *our* judgements, true relative to our standards and our criteria, but *objectively* certain [3.3.1].

The way he seeks to prove that our Clear and Distinct Ideas are objectively true is by showing that our best judgements are guaranteed by God. The proof is discussed in 3.4.1, and its relation to the proofs of God is considered in 3.4.3. Here I want to consider the wider question of whether Descartes' whole anti-sceptical, objectivist project – the attempt to validate human thought as a whole – is in fact intelligible.

1. An Anti-Cartesian Argument

Any attempt to do what Descartes tries to do – to show that human thought can get to the objective truth – must necessarily fail, for the simple reason that the only tool we have with which to do the job is human thought itself. In order to show that human standards work, we would need some independent standpoint from which to assess them. We would need to be able to stand aside from human thought as a whole, and to ask ourselves how, if at all, it connects with reality, with the world itself. But necessarily we can never be in a position to do that, because as humans we can never get outside of the system of human thought in order to validate it. The Vogons could do it, presumably. (Perhaps they are up there now, sniggering in their harsh, Vogon way, about the absurd mismatch between what humans think of as reality and the objective reality itself.) And God of course could do it. And that is why Descartes is forced to appeal to God in his disproof of Scepticism: Descartes tries to show that our best thinking is correct not just by our standards, but also from God's objective point of view. But that manoeuvre can never work, according to this line of thought, because all Descartes can ever give us is *his human perspective* on God's point of view, which is not an independent position at all [3.4.3].

In more general terms, you could put the argument this way: anything which will serve to guarantee human knowledge must either be an instance of human knowledge, or something else. If it is an instance of human knowledge, then it can't do the job because that would be circular: we would be using our knowledge to validate itself. But if the supposed guarantee is *not* itself an instance of human knowledge, then it still couldn't do the job for us, because it would be something we didn't know. Either way, no guarantee is available: if it is something we know, then it can't do the job, and if it's not something we know, it can't help us. So Descartes' strategy must fail, and Scepticism can never be defeated.

Does that work? It seems to me very powerful. If you are impressed by it, then you might also like the following, which points in exactly the opposite direction.

2. Anti-Sceptical Argument

Any attempt to deny that we have objective knowledge must always fail. After all, denying that we have objective knowledge means saying that human thought doesn't work, that human beings have no way of getting to the truth, they are permanently cut off from reality. But how could any human being ever be in a position to draw that conclusion? God or the Vogons could do it, perhaps, but we can't. After all, any evidence to the effect that human beings can't know reality will be either an instance of human knowledge, or something else. If it is an instance of human knowledge, then it can't serve to show that human knowledge doesn't work, because it must necessarily undermine itself: if we accepted the conclusion (there is no knowledge), we would have to reject the premise – the item of knowledge that was our ground for accepting it. On the other hand, if the reason for our Scepticism is *not* itself an instance of human knowledge, then it can never do the job of undermining our belief system, because it is necessarily something we don't know. Either way, Scepticism is indefensible [3.1.9].

Are you convinced?

The two arguments seem to be exactly parallel, so it looks as if they must stand or fall together. Where would that leave us?

It seems to me to show that Scepticism and Certainty go hand-in-hand, and that if one of them makes sense, then so does its opposite.[67] The reason is that both depend on our being able to talk intelligibly of the way the world is in itself, in contradistinction to the way it is for people. We *have* to make sense of such a distinction, if we are to make sense of the idea of genuine, objective certainty – if we want to reassure ourselves that what we hold to be true is not just true by our standards, but true objectively, absolutely or true full stop; but if we *can* make sense of that kind of certainty, then we will have to come to the conclusion that it is necessarily unattainable.

Or to put it another way, only by denying the distinction between reality-for-us and Reality Full Stop can we achieve Descartes' aim of producing a final disproof of Scepticism; but by doing so we will have cut ourselves off from any possibility of the kind of certainty he was looking for [3.1.2].

Links

- For the Hyperbolical Doubt, and Descartes' answer to it, see 3.3.1 and 3.4.1.
- This anti-sceptical, anti-objectivist line of thought also comes up in 3.1.9, 3.1.10 and 3.4.3.

3.4.5 DISCUSSION 19

DESCARTES AND SCIENCE: REASON, EXPERIENCE AND THE POSSIBILITY OF SCIENTIFIC KNOWLEDGE

The story I am trying to tell in this book is that the purpose of the *Meditations* was to demonstrate that what we would call 'scientific' knowledge is

1. Possible
2. Certain
3. The *only* path to secure knowledge of the world, and
4. Compatible with, and indeed inseparable from, the knowledge and worship of God.

That opinion is far from uncommon among Descartes commentators these days. Yet it flies in the face of many years of philosophical work on the subject, where the dominant view was that Descartes downplayed the importance of scientific knowledge, or even held it to be impossible. The reasons for that strange view (after all, this is a man who wrote books on Anatomy, Animal Reproduction, Cosmology, Light, Meteorology, Optics, and Psychology, and whose greatest and most famous work was on Physics) go deep in the history of philosophy in the English-speaking world [4.2], but there are two features of what we have seen in the *Meditations* that might be taken to support it, and that need to be explained if we are to see what the book is really about.

1. Throughout the *Meditations*, Descartes works hard to convince us that we should turn our attention away from sensory knowledge, and that only knowledge based on *a priori* certainties – on Clear and Distinct Ideas – is really immune from doubt, or is really knowledge at all. But science, we all know, is based on observations, that is, on sensory knowledge.

Doesn't that mean Descartes has a very low opinion of scientific knowledge?

2. The whole project of the *Meditations* is to find *certainty* – knowledge that is fixed and unchanging and beyond doubt. But science does not deal in such currency: science is not a body of unchanging truth, but an ongoing inquiry. Our best theories explain the knowledge we have acquired; but as that knowledge base changes and expands, those theories must be refined, adapted, or abandoned as appropriate. Scientific knowledge is, therefore, always *revisable*, in a way that Descartes' model of knowledge cannot allow.[68]

1. Science and Reason

I argued in 3.4.5 that Descartes is perfectly well aware that scientific knowledge begins with observation. But that is exactly his point: that it *begins* there. But it has to go far beyond observation in order to become scientific. That is what he thinks his opponents, the Aristotelians, fail to do: because they merely collect and classify observations, and don't try to look beyond appearances to a deeper level of reality in order to see what is really going on, they can never achieve genuine and lasting knowledge, however 'accurate' their purely observational knowledge might be. And the element that is missing from their investigations, the *real* basis of scientific knowledge, is not its starting-point in experience, but the factor which transforms observations into science, and that factor is *reason*.

Descartes doesn't give us any detailed account of the interrelations of reason and experience in the development of scientific knowledge, but here is a simple model, articulated and named much later, which fits with both his practice and his theory of the subject. The model is called the Hypothetico-Deductive Model (HDM) of scientific reasoning, and since at least the nineteenth century it has been seen by many people as the basic form of scientific thinking and scientific method.

According to the HDM, what the scientist does is first to make observations in his field of study (I say 'his', because when this model was invented all scientists were thought to be, and most of them were, male), and then to try and come up with a theory, an hypothesis, which would explain them. For example, Edmund Halley collected records of sightings of comets through the ages, and in 1705 he put forward the hypothesis that they were Newtonian objects moving in elongated elliptical orbits. At this point we don't yet have science being done: we have some observations, and an educated guess. The science begins when he *works out*, on the basis of his theory, how it could be tested – what observable consequences would follow if it were true (or what he can 'deduce' from his 'hypothesis' – hence the name). In this case he concluded that if he was right, the comet would return in 1758. If it had not in fact arrived, his theory would have been shown to have been false; but when it duly did arrive, his theory was confirmed, and the comet has been known as Halley's Comet ever since. (Unfortunately, as luck would have it, Halley had died before he was immortalized.)

Descartes' epistemology, it seems to me, is consistent with the account of scientific thinking that the HDM later provided. By the end of Meditation 4 he has – to his own satisfaction, at least – *proved* that the kind of rational judgement that is involved in such inquiries is guaranteed to get at the truth, and therefore that if we follow the path of scientific reasoning (if we give our assent only to Clear and Distinct Ideas), we need never go astray.

2. Science and Certainty

It has often been pointed out that scientists following the HDM would be able to disprove false theories, but not to prove true ones. That is a simple point of logic: if I deduce from my theory that X will happen, and it doesn't happen, then my theory *must* be wrong; my hypothesis is falsified, disproved. But if X *does* happen, then all I have shown is that my theory *could* be true – there is always at least an outside chance that X happened for some other reason, and I just got lucky. My hypothesis may be *confirmed*, but it can never be *proved*.[69] Does that mean that because Descartes seeks knowledge which is absolutely certain he can't be advocating natural science as conceived on the lines of the HDM?

No. When Descartes claims that God guarantees our Clear and Distinct Ideas, and therefore that we can't go wrong if we give our assent only to ideas we conceive Clearly and Distinctly, he isn't talking about scientific *theories*, but about scientific *reasoning*. In the example I gave above, the Clear and Distinct Ideas involved are not Halley's claim that his comet follows an elliptical orbit, but the *inferences* that he makes to the effect that *if* he is right, *then* the comet will return in 1758; that *if* the comet returns as predicted, *then* his theory will be confirmed, and that *if* it doesn't appear, *then* his theory will have been falsified. It is that ability to make rational inferences that Descartes believes is, if applied carefully, guaranteed to find the truth.

That surely seems a natural, relatively uncontroversial account of the matter. And it is perfectly compatible with the suggestion that Halley might have got it wrong. If we had later decided that comets are all in fact meteorological events in the earth's atmosphere, and that the 1758 sighting was not the return of the comet, but the visit of an alien spaceship, then we would say that poor old Halley had got it wrong. But he was wrong because his data were wrong, because there were alternative explanations which he hadn't thought of, *not* because the rational judgements – the Clear and Distinct Ideas – that led him to his conclusions were themselves at fault. Those inferences, if we do them properly, *can't* go wrong. And that simple fact together with the centrality of such inferences in scientific reasoning are what Descartes is aiming to convince us of.

Descartes, then, does not have an 'a priorist', anti-empirical, anti-scientific 'rationalist' epistemology.[70] He knows as well as we do that the facts of nature cannot be discovered *a priori* by philosophers sitting in their stove-heated rooms,[71] but must be derived from and tested against empirical evidence. And he knows as well as we do that although the kind of logical inference which is involved in scientific thinking is itself beyond question, the conclusions we derive from those inferences do not have the same certainty. But I wouldn't want to give the impression that his attitudes to these questions are just the same as our own. There are at least three differences between Descartes' position and that of a contemporary advocate of the HDM, and these have played a part in the misrepresentation of him through the years.

1. Many people nowadays say science is based on 'the facts of experience', or 'empirical data' which have some kind of unquestionable, foundational status. Descartes thinks *all* empirical evidence is superficial, potentially misleading, and has to be interpreted by the intellect. He thinks the Doubt of Meditation 1 has proved that claim, by showing that *no*

experience is absolutely certain. Is he right? Or do you think there are empirical facts?[72]

2. Descartes thinks the scientific theories he has produced, while they are not themselves Clear and Distinct Ideas, are so well confirmed and so well argued for that they are almost as certain as the logic that he employs in arriving at them. He says they have the same status as if you had a long text written in code, and eventually discovered a key which made perfect sense of the whole thing. In those circumstances, it would always be logically possible that you had the wrong key, and that it was just a coincidence that you managed to make sense of every word in the text; but your theory would be *practically* (*moraliter/morale*) certain, and no-one in their right minds would doubt that they had found the right answer (*Principles*, 4.205).[73]

For Descartes, then, the truth about the nature of the world and our place in it is a closed body of knowledge which can be unlocked, and to which he thinks he has found the key. Is that how we see things?

It seems to me that much of the time we speak in just that way. We talk of scientific 'knowledge', and scientific 'proof'; we say 'modern science has shown that . . .' or 'we have now discovered that . . .', and many people treat theories such as Evolution, the Big Bang or Gene Theory in just the way Descartes describes: as codes we have now managed to crack. Theoretically they could be mistaken, but for all practical purposes we treat them as known *facts*.

At the same time, though, we seem also to subscribe to a very different view of the matter. Science, we say, is a never-ending adventure, an ever-changing body of revisable theories, evolving and developing as our understanding grows. According to this way of thinking, there is no such thing as a *true* scientific theory, only the best we have at present; there is properly speaking therefore no such thing as scientific *knowledge*, unless it means knowledge of what is currently believed – all we really have is our current collection of interconnected theories and practices, which we regard as better than any rival, but not as the final word.

It seems to me that those two positions are quite incompatible. Do you agree? If so, which do you think is correct?

Are you going to be a Cartesian, or are you willing to abandon the belief in scientific knowledge?

3. The third difference is that Descartes thinks the work of science is inseparable from an understanding of God's purposes and of the true nature and duties of human beings [3.3.9]. We tend to think that religion and morality only get in the way of scientific progress. Which is right?

Links

- The kind of Aristotelian science Descartes is rejecting is set out in 3.1.11.
- The question of scientific knowledge is closely related to that of Objectivity – see Chapter 2 and 3.6.5.

PART V: THE NATURE OF MATTER, AND
THE CERTAINTY OF GOD

3.5.1 MEDITATION 5, SECTION 1. (63–5)

THE KNOWLEDGE OF MATTER

Overview

So now I've established a means of reaching the truth, and I understand what mistakes are, and how to avoid them. There's a lot still
to find out, but the most pressing task is to see if I can resolve my
doubts about the material world. And before I can settle the question
of whether there is such a thing, I need to get clear about exactly
what it is I'm talking about (63).

When I think of the world around me just in terms of shapes,
sizes, numbers, motions and durations, I have a clear grasp of it,
and that mathematical view of it comes naturally to me (63–4).

And more importantly, the categories in terms of which that
understanding is constructed – like for example the idea of a
triangle – are things about which I can have certain knowledge *even
if no such things exist in nature*. I don't acquire such concepts from
experience, and I don't make them up (64–5).

Commentary

By the end of the *Meditations*, The Thinker will have rebuilt the
house of knowledge from the ground up (*Discourse*, 2.VI.13–14),
or put all the sound apples back in her barrel of beliefs, with the
rotten ones removed (OR7, 481) – in other words, she will have
removed all her mistaken common-sense beliefs and inherited
opinions, and replaced them with a secure and lasting knowledge of God, herself and the world. Because of that, it is easy on
reading the book to get the impression that when she gets to the
end she thinks she's back where she started: that she's fought off
the Sceptical doubts she had raised, and reassured herself (and
us, if we follow her), that after our shared retreat we can go back
to the familiar world we stepped out of 6 days earlier, reassured
that our knowledge of it is no dream or illusion.

But that is not at all the effect Descartes is aiming for. After
a successful retreat, after all, one hopes to go back to find the

world renewed, to see it with different eyes, to have a completely different perspective on things. And that is just how Descartes wants you to emerge from reading the *Meditations*. He hopes you will have learned to replace the corrupt, error-strewn, unreliable, all-too-human child's-eye-view of your sensory involvement in the world with the pure, intellectual, secure, objective, semi-divine understanding of the Man of Reason, or the Man of Science, who knows the world not with the eyes of the body, but with the eye of the mind. And if you can do that, then the world that he will give back to you in Meditation 6 when he finally gets round to proving the existence of matter will be a very different place from the one you left via the Doubt of Meditation 1. And here in Meditation 5 is where he sets out those differences.

1. The nature of matter

The material world whose existence was put in doubt in Meditation 1 was the familiar world of day-to-day experience – the world of trees and flowers and people and mountains and rivers and the dirt under your fingernails. The world that Descartes will eventually give back to us is a very different place: it is the material continuum that his mechanist science sees as the explanation for all physical phenomena, governed by the three deterministic laws of mechanical interaction [3.2.4]. That means that unlike the world of experience it is a place without separate physical objects, or chance or empty spaces; a world without colours, or tastes or values; without sounds, or beauty or importance. It is a world which *we perceive* in all those different ways, of course, but which in itself is completely describable with no mention of them, in terms only of its mechanical 'Primary Qualities' – its shapes, sizes, numbers and motions – all of which can and should be expressed in purely mathematical terms [3.2.5; 3.6.5].

2. The knowledge of matter

Two things to notice here. *First*, as we have seen before, that our sensory knowledge of the material world has to be replaced by the non-sensory, purely intellectual, mathematical understanding that is as near as we can get to God's own timeless understanding of his ongoing creative activity. *Second*, the perhaps surprising suggestion that our certain knowledge of the material world is completely independent of the question of whether that world really exists or not.

That second point is an important feature of Descartes' position that it's easy to miss. It seems very strange to say that the defeat of Scepticism occurs in Meditation 4, with the proof of God's non-deceiving nature [3.4.1], when we are unsure of the existence of the material world right up until the end of Meditation 6. Yet that is clearly the structure of the train of thought that Descartes sets out, and which he expects us to find compelling. But how can that work? Surely, the existence of a real world around us is something so obvious, so fundamental to our understanding of things and of what we are, that if we can't be sure of that, we can't be sure of *anything*?

But think about it. What position have we reached by this stage? *If* you had followed the train of thought to this point, and you were convinced by Descartes' proof that our Clear and Distinct Ideas must be true, but hadn't found any combination of Clear and Distinct Ideas which would show that the material world exists, what, if anything, would you know?

The basic point is what we saw in Meditation 1, when *a priori* knowledge survived the Dream Doubt. The Thinker came to the conclusion then that she could still rely on the whole of mathematics, and on all conceptual truths about the natures of things [3.1.4]. But now that we have clarified its nature and secured its basis, how far can such conceptual knowledge take us?

The surprising answer is that Descartes can plausibly claim that it reaches the whole of natural science. What, after all, does science aim to know? The answer, surely, is the *natures* of things. Physics, for example, aims to reveal the nature of matter: what it is in itself, and how it operates. But the *nature* of matter is something we can know independently of the question of whether or not matter actually *exists*, just as we can know the nature of a triangle even if we don't know there actually are any triangles in existence.

'But surely', I hear you cry, 'the two cases aren't the same. The nature of a triangle it is plausible to say we can know *a priori*: if you have enough experience of the world to understand the concept of a triangle, you can work out a lot of its properties just by a process of inference, without the need to examine any actual triangles. But Physics isn't concerned only with the *idea* of matter and what can be deduced from it. Even if we grant Descartes the suggestion that thought experiments like that of the piece of wax [3.2.3] can show that in its basic nature matter is just extended stuff, completely describable by its Primary Qualities, that will only be a beginning. Physics also needs to know hard empirical facts about how matter behaves – things like his three Laws of Motion, or his work in Optics and Meteorology – which can't be worked out from the definition of matter, but depend on actual observations of the material world itself!'

Quite true. There is no doubt that natural science seeks to know more about the world than can be worked out *a priori*, and has to derive its conclusions from experience, from observations. But the strange-sounding point is that the material world doesn't actually have to exist in order for us to have experience of it.

Again, the point is only the same as The Thinker made way back in Meditation 1, when she accepted that the Dream Argument shows that the material world might not exist: the fact that I'm having these experiences doesn't prove there is a material world. But if that's true, it means that I can have knowledge of my experiences quite independently of my knowledge of the existence of matter. And that means that all the observations I need for a complete science of the material world are available to me even if that world doesn't in fact exist.[74]

If that doesn't make sense, read the Discussion of Idealism and see if it gets any clearer [3.5.4].

3.5.2 MEDITATION 5, SECTION 2. (65–8)

THE 'ONTOLOGICAL' ARGUMENT FOR GOD
Overview

But just as I can know for certain those properties of a triangle which are included in its nature or definition, so I can also know that God exists, because existence is included in the nature or definition of God. So God exists as certainly as a triangle has three sides (65–6).

That looks like some kind of trick; but it isn't. A thing that didn't exist wouldn't be perfect; God is by definition perfect, so God can't not exist. I can no more think of God as not existing than I can think of a triangle whose interior angles don't add up to 180 degrees (66–7). Of course, I don't have to think of God, or of a triangle, at all; but if

I *do* think carefully about a triangle, I can see what its interior angles must be. And if I think carefully about God, I can see he must exist and must be unique (67–8).

Commentary

Both of Descartes' arguments for the existence of God start from the *concept* of God – necessarily, because given the situation in which The Thinker comes up with them, the only things she can use as a starting point are her own mind, and the ideas in it. The Meditation 3 proof starts from the fact of *The Thinker's having* the idea of God; this one begins with the bare *content* of that idea – from the properties which anything which is going to be called 'God' must necessarily have.[75]

Most people, when they first come across this argument, think it's obviously a mistake, some kind of a trick. As Descartes himself says: '[a]t first sight . . . this is not transparently clear, but has some appearance of being a sophism' (66). Most people also find it very hard to say *why* it doesn't work, or where the trick lies – and the fact that it has been talked about now for almost a thousand years suggests that if it is a trick, it's at least a very clever one.[76]

The basic idea is very simple. God is by definition wholly perfect: he has no weaknesses, no failings, no imperfections. In Anselm's words, God is 'that than which no greater can be conceived'. Of course, you may not think of God that way – you may think of God as just a kind old man in the sky, for example – but then you don't know what God is, what the term 'God' really means,[77] or at least you aren't using the term in the same way as Descartes is, and so you wouldn't be disagreeing with him if you said 'God doesn't exist'. But if you *do* use the term in Descartes' way, then to say 'God doesn't exist' would surely be contradictory: a non-existent thing isn't wholly perfect, because it doesn't exist; it is clearly lacking in something, because it lacks existence; and it is not 'that than which no greater can be conceived', because you can easily conceive of something like it but which *did* exist, and that would be greater, or more perfect or more complete. So to say 'God doesn't exist' means, if properly understood, something like 'the wholly perfect thing isn't wholly perfect', or 'the thing which lacks nothing lacks existence', or 'you can think of something greater than the greatest thing you can think of' – any of which is as crazy as saying that a pink thing isn't coloured, or a triangle doesn't have three sides, isn't it?

Links

- The argument is discussed in 3.5.5.

3.5.3 MEDITATION 5, SECTION 3. (68–71)

THE END OF THE DOUBT

Overview

The existence of God would be obvious if we weren't distracted by life in the sensory world. And the knowledge of God saves us from doubt about other things we are certain of (69–70). So now I can be confident of my knowledge of the physical world. 'But what about the fact that I make mistakes, or the thought that I might be dreaming?' I don't make mistakes about things I Clearly and Distinctly understand, and even if the material world didn't exist, I would still be certain that my physics was true (70–1).

Commentary

This section neatly summarizes Descartes' epistemology, and the train of thought of the *Meditations* to date. The Doubt involved the Error Argument (which The Thinker dismissed), the Dream Argument [3.1.3] and the Nature Argument [3.1.5]. The *Cogito* survived them all [3.2.1], and gave us confidence in our Clear and Distinct Ideas [3.1.1]. Clear and Distinct Ideas gave us God [3.3.4], and God defeated the Nature Argument and showed that confidence in our Clear and Distinct Ideas was not misplaced [3.4.1]. And with that, most of the work is now done: the defeat of the Nature Argument proves that we *can* have objective knowledge of things, even if we haven't yet gone on to defeat the Dream Argument and show that there is a material world corresponding to our physical knowledge [3.5.1]. That position is neatly summed up here, with a re-capitulation of the disproof of Scepticism and a statement of the Platonic or Idealist conclusion.

What the summary makes clear is that the real doubt for Descartes, the one he thinks really threatens our view of ourselves as able to have objective knowledge both of ourselves and of the world around us, is not the more famous and attention-grabbing Dream Doubt, but the Nature Argument, which is defeated by the proof of God's veracity. If that proof doesn't work, he says, then we can 'never have true and certain knowledge about anything, but only shifting and changeable opinions' (69). An atheist, therefore, can never escape from the Nature Argument, and so can never be sure of anything at all. But by an atheist, of course, as the Ontological Argument shows, we can only mean someone who doesn't understand the concept of God.

***

Meditation 4 had shown the theoretical possibility of objective knowledge through the rational analysis of experience. In Meditation 5 The Thinker has fleshed out that possibility in two important ways:

1. She has given an outline description of what the world is like when considered objectively, as it is in itself; and
2. She has made clear that far from undermining the claims of religion, the objective view both entails and is entailed by the necessary existence of God: we can objectively see that God must exist, and until we realize that fact we can have no objective knowledge at all.

3.5.4 DISCUSSION 20

IDEALISM

1. Descartes and Idealism

Descartes establishes the possibility of secure and lasting knowledge prior to and independently of his attempt to prove that there is a material world. And it is clear that at that stage he thinks his knowledge is not restricted to the pure *a priori* certainties of logic and mathematics, but that it extends also to the rational analysis of his experience, and therefore includes the pure science of nature [3.5.1; 3.4.5]. If that seems weird, what it shows is the coherence of Philosophical Idealism.

The first thing to note on this subject is that the term 'Idealism' is used in a whole range of different ways. Its most common use suggests a rather optimistic, impractical attitude: it is used of people who are thought to be more concerned with how things could or should be than with how they actually are. But that is only indirectly connected to its philosophical uses. In Philosophy, Idealism is any one of a range of positions in ontology – in accounts of what exists, or what there is [3.2.9] – to the effect that what exists is rather more mental ('ideal') than most of us nowadays think.

Descartes is not an Idealist. He thinks there exists a real material universe, and he tries to prove that in Meditation 6. But because he thinks that knowledge of the *nature* of matter can be acquired independently of knowledge of the *existence* of matter, he is closer to Idealism than many people think; and he opens the door to positions which are much more Idealist, such as those of Malebranche and Berkeley.[78] Here I am going to give an outline of a simple Idealist position to try to show that Descartes' Idealist tendencies are not as crazy as they may look. (Or failing that, at least to show that other people have been crazier.)

2. The Unassailability of Idealism

Think for a moment about your knowledge of a material thing – say, the book in front of your eyes. Don't think about *the book*, think about *your knowledge* of it. What does it consist in? How do you know the book is there?

Well, you can see it, you can feel it, you remember picking it up and looking at it; you can see its shadow, and the hollow it makes in the silk cushion on which you have reverentially placed it; your neighbour is impressed by it; your cat tries to pee on it. And so on, and so on. All those experiences, and indefinitely many more, are what your awareness of the book consists in. The book itself, of course, is none of those things: it is an independently existing material object, which *causes* all those different experiences, but is not itself *identical to* any of them. And that is no more than a restatement of the point of the Dream Doubt of Meditation 1: that there seems to be no guarantee that I couldn't have all those experiences even if the book itself didn't actually exist.

When we first come across that gap between what there is and what we know of it, it strikes most people as a worry. If I could have all these experiences and yet the object not be there, then how can I claim to know anything about it? Indeed, how can

I claim to know *anything*? The world around me seems to wobble at the thought, as if it loses a dimension I hadn't previously noticed that it had.

But consider. What if one day that problem were solved? Imagine someone invented the Wonderful Matter Detector (or WMD, for short) which you could carry around with you and which (as long as you remembered to put the batteries in) was guaranteed to display a reassuring green light whenever it found itself within 100 metres of a material object. Then you could read Meditation 1 without fear: every time you thought you might be dreaming, you could just pull out your WMD, smile smugly at the little green light and go back to your life, reassured.

But imagine also that with the help of our WMDs we were able to discover the existence of an Evil Demon with the power to destroy matter. This demon could temporarily destroy the whole material world without making any difference to our lives – the lights on our WMDs would all change from green to red, of course, but in other respects everything would be as before. We might discover that the Demon did this for 10 minutes every Saturday afternoon, and occasionally also on Wednesdays, before 2 p.m. How would that discovery make you feel? Of course, Evil Demons being what they are (just as God is constant and unchanging, demons are necessarily fickle and unreliable), we might find that it didn't always keep to a regular pattern, and if we watched our WMDs carefully we would see that matter was flicking in and out of existence all the time. Question: Would you care?

It seems pretty obvious that you wouldn't.

In reality, of course, the WMDs were just a fantasy. (You might say they were just something I made up to get you to agree with me.) In the situation I have imagined, we would just throw the things away, on the grounds that even if we believed them (which we wouldn't), these expensive gadgets with their constantly flickering lights would be completely useless to us. Would we behave in any way differently during the periods when the lights were red than we did when they were green? Would we refuse to go out, or to drink cocoa, on the grounds that the lights are red, so matter doesn't currently exist? Would we during those periods stop talking about all the books and flowers and teapots and so on that weren't currently existing, and talk only about our continuing experiences of them? Or would we go on exactly as before?

It seems obvious to me that we'd behave as if *nothing had changed*: we would handle and talk about the teapots and the rest just as we had before. But if that is true, what would you say if one day you stopped to ask yourself what it *meant* when you said 'Look at that fine teapot' during a period when the lights were red?

The answer, presumably, would be that you wouldn't at that time be talking about the independently existing material object that had recently gone out of existence, but about the consistent sets of teapot experiences you were nevertheless continuing to enjoy. In other words, you would be forced to give an *Idealist* account of teapots. You would say 'When I say it's a real teapot, I don't mean there is a really existing material object, only that the teapot aspects of my life experiences are consistent and unchanged; and when I say "That's not a real teapot, it's a mirage caused by my being forced to go without tea for too long", what I mean is that the usual pattern of my teapot experiences is broken and unreliable: visually it's just the same, but when I try to touch it I feel nothing, and when I try to make tea in it I pour boiling water all over the cat.'

To put the idea more formally, an Idealist of this simple kind says that material objects are actually just sets of experiences (or 'sense data', or 'ideas') in perceiving minds. And where do those experiences come from? What causes them, if not the material objects we used to believe in? According to Berkeley, the answer is God, who puts the ideas directly into our minds; according to later versions of essentially the same story, the question makes no sense, because you are trying to talk about things ('material objects', 'God') which by definition are not experiences – and terms which are not in the end translatable into statements about experiences have no meaning.[79]

You may think neither of those answers is satisfactory. But two points need to be made.

1. This Idealist story is frustratingly difficult to refute, because every bit of evidence that we take to show the existence of matter counts equally well for the Idealist, and necessarily *nothing* that you can ever experience can possibly count against her. So if you are going to refute Idealism and prove the existence of matter, you will need some argument like

that which Descartes provides. Do you have one? And is your belief in matter only as strong as that argument?

2. The Idealist story has one great advantage over our common-sense belief in matter. If we take our words to refer to material objects, but we can't prove that they exist, then we seem to be stuck for ever in External World or 'Cartesian' Scepticism [3.1.7]. If the only reality is the reality of experiences, that problem seems to disappear.[80]

3.5.5 DISCUSSION 21

CAN GOD NOT EXIST? THE 'ONTOLOGICAL' ARGUMENT

A lot has been written about the Ontological Argument for God of Meditation 5. To help you to make up your mind about it, I want to explain here what I think is the most famous and the most powerful attempt to show why it doesn't work; and then to say why I think the question isn't quite that simple.

I tried in the Commentary to explain how the argument is supposed to work: if we analyse the idea of God – the nature, definition or 'essence' of God, what properties God has to have in order to be God – we can see, according to Descartes, that it entails that God exists.

The idea that what follows from something's essence is necessarily true of it seems unobjectionable. Because a triangle is defined as a plane figure with three straight sides, you can *prove* that its interior angles must add up to 180 degrees: given what a triangle is, it *has* to have that property. Of course, there may not be any triangles in existence, but if there are, then just in virtue of being triangles, they must have that property. Descartes claims that God is unique in that his essence involves his *existence*: that given what it is to be God, God must necessarily exist.

There are many ways of trying to resist that conclusion.[81] Probably the most famous is that of Immanuel Kant (1724–1804). According to Kant, what I called the 'trick' of the Ontological Argument lies in the fact that the grammar of existence-statements is misleading. Grammatically, the statements 'Pigs can fly', 'Pies are tasty' and 'God exists' are all alike. In each case a predicate ('can fly', 'are tasty', 'exists') is applied to a subject (pigs, pies, God). But although the three statements are grammatically the same, *logically* the last one is very different from the first two, because although 'can fly' and 'are tasty' are genuine, logical predicates – properties which things can either have or lack – 'exists' is quite different. Existence isn't a *property* which some things have and some things lack: if something doesn't exist, it isn't a thing which lacks existence, it just isn't a *thing* at all.[82]

Think of it this way. Although it looks like it, in reality the statement 'God exists' isn't a statement about God at all. Rather than being a statement about God, telling us that he exists, it is a statement about the world, about reality, telling us that it contains God. Its logical form is better represented not as 'God exists', but as 'There is a God', or 'Reality includes God'.

The point of that seemingly trivial, technical remark is what happens when you negate these various statements. The Ontological Argument turns on the claim that it would be a contradiction to say 'God doesn't exist'. But if existence isn't a predicate, then to say 'God doesn't exist' isn't to say of the all-perfect God that he lacks the perfection of existence, but only to say of the world that it doesn't contain an all-perfect being. And there is no contradiction in saying 'Reality contains no all-perfect being', or 'There is no God'.

Does that make sense?

It's probably true to say that the majority of philosophers nowadays take Kant to have decisively refuted the Ontological Argument.[83] The victory doesn't come without its costs, though. First, you have to accept the idea of Logical Form: that there is a Real Meaning of the statement 'God exists' which the grammar of the sentence obscures. That move is essential to the refutation. (It would lose all its force if Kant merely said 'I prefer to analyse the sentence *this* way'.) But not everyone would admit that facts of meaning exist in that way. Second, it causes problems for our understanding of non-existent objects because it seems to mean that non-existent things have no properties. But that would mean it isn't true to say that Sherlock Holmes lived in Baker Street, Gandalf fought a balrog and Little Miss Muffet sat on a tuffet. But it is, isn't it?

But here's a question of a quite different kind. If we grant that Kant's refutation works, does it work equally well for any conception of God?

The thought I am having is that if God is a being, a thing in the world, then the refutation carries a lot of weight. But is that what Descartes' God is meant to be? It seems to me that both Anselm and Descartes think of God not as just a being (albeit one of a very special kind), but as Being. That is very clear in Anselm, for whom God is the indescribable One, the only Reality, which shows itself with varying degrees of clarity in everything that, as we say in everyday language, exists. And in so far as Descartes believes that God is the only substance, the one reality which underlies all the appearances of the world, his view is perhaps not too far removed from Anselm's neo-Platonic vision [3.3.9]. Does Kant's refutation work equally well for such a strange, alien conception?

The refutation turns on the claim that while grammatically there may be a contradiction in saying 'God doesn't exist', there is no contradiction in saying 'There is no God', which is in fact the true form of the statement. But is that still true if God is the only reality? The statement 'God doesn't exist' would then be equivalent to 'There is no reality', or 'Reality has the following form: there is no reality' – which looks again like a contradiction.

If that makes any sense, then what it shows is what, perhaps, we should have known all along. The question of the existence or non-existence of God, like all complex and contested questions, is not a simple one which we might hope to settle by a single argument, one way or the other, but a question of the coherence and usefulness, or otherwise, of a mass of interconnected concepts, beliefs and attitudes.

Links

- Different kinds of atheism are set out in 3.3.7.
- Descartes' conception of God as the single true substance is explained in 3.3.9.

PART VI: THE EXISTENCE OF MATTER

3.6.1 MEDITATION 6, SECTION 1. (71–8)

UNDERSTANDING AND IMAGINATION
Overview

Now that I've got clear what I know of the *nature* of matter, I need to ask about its *existence*. I know matter *could* exist; and it *looks and feels* as though it exists; but does it really (71–2)?

We have to separate my understanding of the world from the mental images that often accompany it. The images aren't essential parts of my mind, as my intellect is. It may well be that they are generated in my material body, and then grasped by my mind. But there is nothing about such images which *proves* that I have a body (72–3).

My sensory view of the world is rich and varied, though confused. Do the senses show that matter exists? I'll have to review the chain of thought I have followed, to get clear what I now think (74).

I started out thinking I was one physical object among many, that the nature of objects was revealed by the nature of my experiences, and that all my knowledge came from my senses. But really there is no resemblance between the sensations I have and their causes, and eventually I realized that the senses are misleading. And then I worked out that I could dream anything I could experience, and I thought that my nature might be such that I go wrong all the time. What do I think now (74–8)?

Commentary

The job of Meditation 6 is to complete the account of the world and our place in it which Descartes is offering us in exchange for the common-sense view with which The Thinker set off on her retreat [3.5.1]. In order to do that there are three things it has to do: to show that the matter we have now come to understand does actually exist; to finish the argument for the immateriality of the mind begun in Meditation 2 [3.2.2], and to explain how the latter has knowledge of the former. The first of those is done in what I call Section 3, the second in Section 2; here and in Section 4 he explains the interrelations of mind and world.

Imagination

When I think of a triangle, I tend to *visualize* a triangle: a rather vague mental *image* comes to my mind. It has no particular colour, or background, or even size. It is roughly equilateral, and the lines that make it up are quite thick, perhaps even three-dimensional. As far as I know, every time I think about my concept of a triangle the same or a very similar image comes to mind, but I'm not sure about that. *Your* image is probably very different – if you even have one.

Descartes' point is that the occurrence of this kind of mental imagery – which he calls 'imagination' – is nothing to do with my *concept* of a triangle, with my *understanding* of what a triangle is. And he tries to prove as much with the example of a chiliagon (72): I understand the difference between a thousand-sided figure and a ten-thousand-sided figure perfectly well; but the *image* that comes to mind when I think of either of them is the same – just a vague shape with a lot of sides, looking like a circle from a distance {OR 5, 384–5}.

That seems to me like a good argument. We might add that different people have very different images associated with the same concept, even when they understand it in much the same way, and also that most of the concepts I possess (mistake, Wednesday, useful) on most occasions don't actually evoke *any* images in my mind at all – though I could perhaps invent some if I tried. Surely, the having of this kind of image is not what thinking of the things in question consists in, but just an extra feature that is an interesting – and some might argue important – part of many people's mental lives.

For Descartes these images are essentially *bodily* events. When I actually *see* a triangle an image is formed on my retina, and that image eventually produces a particular kind of brain event. Because of the close connection between my mind and my body, my mind is sensitive to the new brain-state which is thereby produced: its awareness of it takes the form of a distinct feeling to which it can turn its attention [3.2.6].

Now, the link between that feeling and the object which ultimately caused it is actually quite a remote one. The same feeling can be caused by something else (e.g. when I *dream* of a triangle, or *hallucinate*), and although that feeling is *characteristic* of my body's response to triangles – for example, it is quite different from what it feels like to perceive a circle or a square – it isn't any kind of accurate *representation* of the thing that produced it. In fact it is no more and no less *accurate* as a representation of the nature of the triangle than are the very different *touch* sensations which the blind person with a stick gets on encountering the same thing. Those tactile 'images' or 'impressions' are equally characteristic of the object's shape, but they don't in any way resemble it; and neither do our visual images. Both sets of sensations are just our mind's awareness of brain-states whose character is specific to a particular kind of cause.

So what is that cause, the triangle, *really* like, if it isn't like my image of it? The answer is the mathematical physicist's description of the area of matter I am reacting to, a description confined to numerical values for sizes, shapes, positions and motions, and containing no *visual* terms at all. As it is in itself, the triangle doesn't actually *look like* anything at all, because the way something *looks* isn't part of what it is in itself, only of how human beings feel when they encounter it.

Imagination and Understanding, then, are very different kinds of mental activity. When the mind understands it just thinks; when it imagines, it attends to states of its body, and consciously interprets the body's (unconscious) reactions. The difference between understanding something and experiencing it is a bit like the way you can either just think of a loved one, or think of them with the help of a photograph to bring them more forcefully to mind. To continue the analogy, imagine a person who didn't understand what a photograph is. On being told it is a likeness of my late Uncle Doug, they assume he was black-and-white, two-dimensional and creased down the middle. That would clearly be a mistake (Uncle Doug was actually one of my more colourful and multi-dimensional relatives, and no more creased than other men of his age) – and it would be exactly the same kind of mistake as that of a person who thinks of the world in sensory terms.

My analogy of course breaks down because most of the time we don't need photographs in order to know the people and things around us, whereas we do need 'imagination' to find out about nature. Descartes is *not* suggesting we can know the world *a priori*; but he *is* saying that our minds have the ability to go beyond imagination, both to form an intellectual grasp of the things around us [3.4.5], and to know things of which we can't have physical sensations – like logic, mathematics and God. Such 'innate' ideas [3.3.2] show that The Thinker was wrong to think 'that I had nothing at all in the intellect which I had not previously had in sensation' (75). My understanding would survive even if I lost the ability to have images, which shows that my imagination is not an essential part of what I am; but my understanding is what enables me to be conscious, even of my mental images, so if I didn't have that, I would not exist at all (73).[84]

Links

- Descartes' 'dualist' account of mind and body is set out in 3.2.6.

3.6.2 MEDITATION 6, SECTION 2. (78)

THE 'REAL DISTINCTION' BETWEEN MIND AND BODY

Overview

Everything I Clearly and Distinctly understand is possible. So if I can Clearly and Distinctly understand one thing without another, that means they *could* exist separately. So the fact that I can Clearly and Distinctly understand my own existence independently of the existence of a body means that my mind and body are Really Distinct, and my mind could exist without my body.

Commentary

A 'Real Distinction' is a kind of technical term, meaning a distinction between *things* (from Latin *res*, a thing), that is, between substances [3.2.9].[85] So to say there is a Real Distinction between Mind and Body is to say that they are different things, or different substances. And a substance, of course, is something that can exist, and can be understood, independently of anything else. Back in Meditation 2 The Thinker came to the conclusion that she could have a Clear and Distinct understanding of herself as something separate from the whole material world, because while she couldn't doubt her own existence, she could doubt away all matter [3.2.2]. At that point she then backs off from concluding that she must, therefore, be a separate thing, Really Distinct from her body, because at that stage she hasn't proved that her Clear and Distinct Ideas are actually *true*. Now that she has done that [3.4.1], she can complete the argument – even though she doesn't yet know whether or not there is a material world for her to be separate *from*. She has shown that she can have a Clear and Distinct Idea of her self which is independent of her idea of matter; and now she knows that it is therefore *true* that her self can exist without matter – that is, that it isn't just a feature of her thinking that she can separate the two ideas, but that they *really are* separate – as philosophers nowadays might say, she claims to have shown that her inability to separate them is not a fact of *psychology*, but of *logic*.[86]

The whole argument is discussed in 3.2.8. Here we see only the final step: that if the two concepts are indeed separate, then it would be possible for God to make a world with the one and not the other, that is, they are different things. Of course, as long as I am alive my mind *doesn't* exist separately from my body – the two are so closely intermingled as in effect to form a single thing, Descartes sometimes says (81; OR4, 228), and his whole account of human life is of the interweaving of those two elements [3.2.6]. But the fact remains that it would be logically possible for one to exist without the other, so they are, or belong to, different things, or different substances, don't they?

3.6.3 MEDITATION 6, SECTION 3. (78–80)

THE EXISTENCE OF MATTER

Overview

My imagination and sensory perceptions depend on my mind, and not vice-versa. Other things I can do – like moving – are not intellectual acts, so they must depend on my body, if I have one. But my ability to perceive sensory images would be no use to me unless there were something which *produced* those images. I don't produce them myself, because they're not intellectual things, and I have no power over when they arise, so they must be caused by something else. That cause must be at least as substantial as matter, so it must be either matter itself, God, or something in-between.

But God has given me a natural inclination to believe it's matter, and God is no deceiver. So my ideas of matter must be caused by matter. The material world may not be as I sense it, but (because my Clear and Distinct Ideas are true) it *must* be as I *understand* it to be {*Principles*, 2.1}.

Commentary

By this stage, we have to remember, Descartes has already proved that he can have stable and lasting knowledge, not only of *a priori* truths, but more importantly of the unchanging laws of nature which underlie and explain the changing phenomena of his experience. He has shown that God exists, and that his ongoing creative activity generates the world that we know; and he has shown that we have the capacity to escape from our sensory awareness of that world to a scientific knowledge of its true nature. And all that even if, contrary to appearances, there is in fact no material world for us to have knowledge of [3.5.1; 3.5.4]. Descartes' theory, in other words, is sufficiently Platonist, close enough to Idealist, not to be severely damaged if he fails to prove the existence of matter.

And that is perhaps just as well, because I don't think many people have ever been very impressed by this argument. The most interesting question, it seems to me, is not how strong it is, but whether we can improve on it.

But the argument is not without some force. Try to think yourself into the position The Thinker has reached at this point. Given that she has convinced herself that God exists and is no deceiver, and that God has given her the wherewithal to know his creation; and given that she, like everyone else, finds it hard to escape from the conviction that she is (at least attached to) a material body in a material world, it is perhaps not unreasonable for her to think that this conviction, which all of us have and which seems to be built into us, can't be a mistake. As Malebranche said,[87] although it seems less than a complete proof, *if* you accept the premises, it does at least seem to offer some support for its conclusion, to make it more likely than not that matter exists.

Its weaknesses as a definitive proof, though, are fairly obvious. First, it can clearly only be as strong as the proof that God exists and is no deceiver, which acts as one of its premises. Second, the reasons The Thinker gives for saying that she is not herself the cause of her sensations look less than compelling. (How does she know they're not intellectual? Does the fact that she can't *choose* them prove she doesn't *cause* them?) Third, it looks weaker than the very similar argument for the truth of Clear and Distinct Ideas in Meditation 4 [3.4.1], in that while it might be hard to see how an all-good God could leave us with no possibility of ever knowing the truth, it seems much less obvious that such a God couldn't let us make mistakes about the existence of matter, especially given what a relatively small part we have just seen that it actually plays in our knowledge of nature.[88] The difference between the two arguments perhaps turns on exactly how 'natural' the belief in matter is, and much of the rest of Meditation 6 is devoted to specifying under what circumstances and to what extent what is natural can be deceptive.[89]

For all those reasons, then, Descartes' proof seems less than convincing. Yet Descartes is surely right that we all feel a natural and almost inescapable conviction that there is a material world around us. Do you have a better argument for that conclusion than the one he offers?

Links

- For a sketch of a world without matter, see 3.5.4.
- On the conclusion to be drawn from the failure of a proof, see 3.3.8.

3.6.4 MEDITATION 6, SECTION 4. (80–END)

THE KNOWLEDGE OF PARTICULAR PHYSICAL FACTS (OR THE END OF THE DREAM)

Overview

So now I know the nature of matter, and I know that it exists. What about my knowledge of particular physical facts (80)?

My mind doesn't *observe* my body, as a sailor observes and monitors what happens in a ship; it *feels* the body's interactions with the world around it, its reactions to them, and its internal drives. We go wrong when we think that those sensations – which are our awareness of the way the body reacts in order to protect and preserve itself – tell us what the world is really like, for example when we think that colour is an inherent property of objects. The senses don't give us the whole picture, and sometimes they mislead us when the usual sensations have unusual causes – for example, when thirst sensations are produced by dropsy and not by the need for water, or when 'phantom limb' sensations are caused by nerve damage and not by the state of the limb in question (80–9).

But now I understand these things, I can see that if I don't take my sensations at face value, but interpret them carefully, they can give me a reliable knowledge of the world which is nothing like the chaos of dream experience. I make mistakes when for practical reasons I have to make a snap judgement, but when I have time to proceed carefully I *can* develop a reliable knowledge of particular facts and events in the world around me (89–90).

Commentary

This final section develops the separation between Understanding and Imagination [3.6.1] to explain why Descartes thinks not only that we can have objective knowledge of the true nature of the world around us but also that we never need to go wrong even about particular facts and events, such as the height of a tree, the cause of an illness, or who killed Cock Robin.

We saw in Meditation 4 [3.4.2] Descartes' explanation of error and his claim that 'it is quite impossible for me to go wrong' if I proceed carefully and (as we would say) scientifically. I argued that we should take that to mean that because Clear and Distinct Ideas can't be doubted, and because God guarantees that what we can't doubt must be true, it follows that in science and metaphysics we can achieve objective knowledge of how things are. But does such knowledge apply only to the unchanging facts of nature, or can it also extend to particular contingent truths?

Descartes' answer is a fairly commonsensical one. The number of factors involved in a particular event like the killing of a robin is actually very large, and the amount of evidence we have might be very small, so there may be practical constraints on whether we can actually find out whodunit. But even here there will be such a thing as a rational, 'scientific' inquiry which will not lead us astray, even if for lack of evidence it cannot give us the answer. The only way we will actually *go wrong* in such a search will be if for lack of time or resources we go beyond what we can establish with certainty (what we perceive Clearly and Distinctly), and make guesses.

The only really new move in this section is the final dismissal of the Dream Doubt, which was the first doubt seriously to damage The Thinker's confidence in her judgements. It was the Dream Doubt which took away her 'natural' belief in the material world [3.1.3], so now that the belief has been reinstated (although the material world he has given us back is very different from the one he took away [3.5.1]), Descartes needs finally to put the doubt to rest.

It is easy to be unimpressed by the way he does it. Most people who think the Dream Doubt raises a problem for our common-sense view of things find that the rebuttal when it finally arrives completely misses the point. All he says is that if we check our experiences against one another and against those from other senses, and if we use our memory to see how each experience fits in to the overall pattern of our lives, then we will easily be able to tell dreams from real life. But surely, if any of our experiences could be a dream, then the other experiences and the memories that we check them against could be dreams as well, couldn't they? Or conversely, if this common-sense response *does* resolve the Doubt, why didn't he just point this out in Meditation 1, and save us all some time?

The answer is that he thinks the Dream Doubt is a worry for The Thinker on Day 1, but not on Day 6. If, like most people, you don't have a carefully worked-out and well-grounded metaphysical and epistemological framework into which to fit your daily life, then you are easily discomfited by doubts like those raised in Meditation 1. The jumble of ill-considered attitudes and half-understood second-hand theories that we pick up in our haphazard passage through life leaves us no defence against serious and persistent questioning. But if you have a carefully thought-out ontology of God and creation, a 'dualist' account of human experience, an explanation of error and an epistemology which says you can attain secure knowledge through the rational interpretation of sensory data, then you should be invulnerable to the kind of panic to which The Thinker succumbs at the start (and to which most readers of the text are still prone). All those things Descartes claims to have put in place by this stage of the story, and all founded on no special training or education, but only on the ability to think things through, which anyone who can read the book must already possess.

The question to ask, in other words, is not whether this argument, as it stands, will solve the Dream Doubt. It won't; but it was never intended to. The question to ask is whether a person who has accepted everything that Descartes has tried to prove since Meditation 1 would have any reason to be worried by the fact that any sensation she has ever felt is one she could in theory feel in a dream. And I don't think she would.

Most of us, though, are not in that happy position, because most of us find that we are *not* convinced by every step of the narrative of the *Meditations*, so that when we read this section our philosophical defences are no stronger than they were at the start. Can you find some other way of firming them up, or should we just accept that our whole world-picture is indefensible?

***

And now the story is complete. In 6 days The Thinker has made the world anew,[90] and she emerges from the retreat with a clear view of herself and her position in the rest of creation. By the end of Meditation 5 she had secured an objective, 'scientific' view of nature through her awareness of and reliance on God, and in Meditation 6 she has completed that story by

1. Securing the existence of the material world we all believe ourselves to inhabit,
2. Demonstrating at the same time our essential independence from that material world, in spite of the entanglement in it which is the defining feature of human life as we know it, and
3. Explaining how as a result reason is able not only to provide true answers to general questions about the world around us, but also to enable us to take an impersonal, objective view of any question whatsoever.

3.6.5 DISCUSSION 22

THE MANIFEST AND THE SCIENTIFIC IMAGE (OR THE BIG QUESTION OF THE *MEDITATIONS* REVISITED)

It has often been pointed out that people in the Modern world – usually taken to mean the West since the seventeenth century – relate to the world, or conceive of the world, in two different ways. On the one hand we think of ourselves as more-or-less stable objects in the world, surrounded by other objects, some of which are like us and some of which are not, and many of which we have learned to recognize and to cope with in ways which most of the time allow us to get on with our lives. We know pretty well what things are dangerous and what things are not, what things we love and what things we don't, what gives us pleasure and what doesn't, what we can do and what we can't. All this practical mastery is no more than the kind of knowledge that any intelligent creature will acquire of its environment, picked up through experience and through what it learns from others.

At the same time, though, we are also able to conceptualize the world in a very different way. We have mastered the technique of abstracting from our lived experience of the world, and indeed from *anyone's* experience of it, so as to think about it in an impersonal, or 'objective' way. Thus the table which I live with, and which I experience as hard and cheap and useful and pale brown but a bit wobbly when extended, I am also able to think of in a way that doesn't relate to any actual experience of it: as consisting largely of empty spaces populated by tiny, fast-moving particles or pressure waves. The sun which I know as warm, bright and yellow I can also think of in non-experiential terms as an unimaginable frenzy of self-sustaining hydrogen fusions. The person I experience as witty and energetic though prone to occasional bouts of temper I can also consider as a complex physical structure driven by uncountable sequences of neuron-firings. And so on, and so on.

These two different conceptions have been familiar to us since early on in our lives, and we skip between them effortlessly as we go through our days. As a result, we easily lose sight of how different the two views are, and of what a major feat of abstraction it is that we engage in so routinely when a hundred times a day we step aside from our experiential grasp of things and think of our world in this impersonal, theory-based, 'objective' way.

Philosophers have characterized this kind of distinction in various ways. Sir Arthur Eddington talked of each object of the familiar world as having a 'scientific duplicate', and famously set out the differences between his 'two tables';[91] Wilfrid Sellars wrote of the contrast between the 'Manifest' and the 'Scientific' images by means of which we conceptualize the world.[92] What is hard for us to realize is that although it seems so natural to us, this double awareness of things is not a permanent, inevitable feature of human consciousness, but seems to be something that came to be a widespread feature of how people confront the world only after the seventeenth century, when it was adopted as part of the reintroduction of broadly Platonic thinking that was an essential part of what we now think of as the beginnings of modern science [Chapter 1].

The story Descartes tells in the *Meditations*, it seems to me, is just his attempt to explain and argue for the difference between the Manifest and the Scientific Image – a distinction which we take for granted, but which most of his contemporaries did not make, and found hard to understand. The world we leave via the Doubt of Day 1 is the Manifest world, the world of subjective, lived experience; the world we re-enter on Day 6 is the Scientific world, the world as seen from the objective standpoint of science [3.5.1]. In Descartes' version, the distinction is that between the carnal world (the world as felt through our awareness of the body's physical responses to its environment) and the intellectual world (the world as grasped by the rational judgements which the mind makes on the basis of its innate power of thinking) [3.6.1; 3.2.6]. It is also the distinction between the human world (the world of the *embodied* mind, entangled with the physical) and the divine world (the world as known to pure intellect) [3.3.9]. It is because we can adopt the Scientific Image that we can achieve objective knowledge; and it is because of the gap between the two images that we face the Hyperbolical Doubt [3.3.1; 3.4.4].

In Chapter 2 I argued that the Big Question which our society has to face is that of non-local criteria for judgements: what do we do when we encounter situations in which what is at issue is not only some particular matter of fact, but also the whole framework by which the truth of that matter of fact might be assessed? Must we say that such problems are insoluble, either because there is no answer or because we have no access to it? Or can we say that there *is* an answer even here, because there exists the possibility of escaping from our personal or our cultural setting and considering the question objectively? Descartes in the *Meditations* argues that we *can* achieve objective knowledge, because we can escape from the Manifest to the Scientific Image of the world.

That seems to me like a very good answer to the question. But as we have just seen, it depends crucially on Descartes' 'dualist' account of human beings, and on his views about God. Take those away, and what are we left with? Can we make sense of an Objective view without them? If the Objective view, the Scientific Image, does *not* mean the view of God, in which the immaterial mind of man has an innate ability to participate, what does it mean?

It seems to me that any point of view, any intelligible perspective on reality, must be *someone's* point of view – if not that of a real person, then that of an imaginary one. That is just what it means to be a point of view, or a perspective: to be intelligible it must make sense in terms of *some* set of standards and values; it must embody *some* specific preconceptions and not others. Descartes obeys that rule, and he makes the idea intelligible as the objective view of God, as shared by the immaterial mind through its innate power of thinking. But take away that setting, and what are you left with?

Without those divine underpinnings, it seems to me, the objective view must necessarily become human again – it becomes merely a view which some of us hold, and others don't. And that means that anyone who thinks (as I do) that it is a valuable point of view, one which is worthy of being widely adopted and shared, will need to find a way of defending it which does not rely on God's help.

CHAPTER 4

RECEPTION AND INFLUENCE OF
THE *MEDITATIONS*

The *Meditations* was a very influential text.

But then, historical influence is a complicated thing. Why did the book get published? Because sufficient and sufficiently influential people thought it should and would be read. And why did people read it? Because they expected to find it interesting, instructive or in some other way beneficial. And when they read it, why did they find Descartes' ideas valuable? Because the book answered their questions, clarified their doubts, reinforced their prejudices, or in some other way connected favourably with their pre-existing attitudes, expectations, beliefs and preferences. The explanation for the *Meditations*' success, in other words, lies not in what it says; it lies in how what it says connected with the minds of its readers. If it is true, therefore, that some of those readers wouldn't have believed what they believed if they hadn't read the book, we mustn't forget that it is also true that none of them would have read it if they hadn't believed what they believed.

When I say that the *Meditations* was influential, then, I am not saying that it single-handedly caused people to think this or that; what I mean is that it expressed ideas which people were able to *use*. And the fact that it has remained an influential work right up to the present day means that people have continued to find a use for it, even after all these years. Inevitably, though, the things it has been useful *for*, the things people have been able to do with it, have changed as time has gone by: as belief systems have shifted and developed, so the ways in which readers have engaged with the text have changed accordingly. Now, the interesting (and confusing) fact is that one of the factors which have produced those changes in peoples' belief systems is the influence of works like the *Meditations*. So what we end up with is a complex kind of circular interaction between the book and its audiences: readers select it as a text they can relate to on the basis of what matters to them and how they see the world; it is significant because the ways in which they use and respond to it are part of the reason why their outlooks change. And those changing attitudes result in our reading the text itself in different ways.

As has often been said, history is more complex than we think.

We have to bear those kinds of complication in mind if we are to make sense of the changing reception of the *Meditations* down the years.

1. THE MEDITATIONS AND HISTORY

The importance of Descartes in the history of Mathematics and Science in the seventeenth century could hardly be overstated. In *Mathematics* he founded Analytic Geometry (the algebraic treatment of curves). In the *Natural Sciences* his impact was enormous, on two different levels.

1. His detailed, practical work in fields such as Cosmology, Meteorology, Anatomy, Biology, Medicine and Optics made him a leading player in every field, a major – often *the* major – contributor, whose work might be contested, but couldn't be ignored.

2. And at least as important as that practical work was the overall physical system within which it was incorporated. Descartes' Mechanism [3.2.4] provided the first plausible overview of the workings of nature as seen by the men of the 'New Philosophy', and although his works were put on the Index of Prohibited Books by the Catholic Church in 1663,[1] it nevertheless became the orthodox model which dominated natural science until the widespread acceptance of a Newtonian view at the end of the century.[2]

But the *Meditations* itself contains none of Descartes' contributions to mathematics or to science, and very little of his overall mechanical system of nature. What it contains instead is the higher-level theorizing which we would now call his *philosophy*. It contains his account of God's relation to creation, and of the nature of human beings and their place in the universe; and at the centre of the picture, but essentially grounded in those first two, is his explanation of how we can achieve objective knowledge of nature through the kind of rational inquiry that we would now call Natural Science. So what can we say about the influence of the *Meditations* in the history of *philosophy*?

The philosophical picture we find in the *Meditations* is also given (with additions and omissions) in the *Principles* and *Discourse*, so it isn't easy to talk about the influence of the one book as opposed to that of the ideas which are presented in all three. But whichever of his works it was known from, it seems to me that the philosophical outlook we find in the *Meditations* has been the most important in Western history,[3] for two reasons. First, all the great thinkers of the second half of the seventeenth century – including Spinoza, Leibniz, Malebranche and Locke – quite consciously took the ideas expressed in the *Meditations* as either their inspiration, their starting-point, their bedrock or their target. When we get to the eighteenth century the explicit references are more often to those successors of Descartes than to the *Meditations* itself, but thinkers like Berkeley and Hume are still very clearly working within a Cartesian framework, and it is only when we come to Kant – who also takes himself in a different way to be resolving the problems that Descartes and his successors had discussed – that we find a major philosopher of whom that is not true.

But the influence of the *Meditations* on other philosophers is only one, and the less interesting, part of the story. The second and much more important part is that the ideas of the *Meditations* have been incorporated into, and have come to dominate, mainstream European thought from Descartes' day to the present.

In saying this I am not suggesting that Descartes changed the course of history, and made us what we are. I think that would be to misrepresent the role of individuals in history in general, and certainly in the history of ideas. Rather, what I think Descartes did was to produce a carefully worked-out set of interconnected ideas which helped people to understand their lives and their place in a changing world. His picture was radical and exciting, it chimed with the rising individualism of the day, it empowered the new lay thinkers against the established and already collapsing intellectual establishment, and it gave a central role to the inventions of the new science while managing to unite it with the religious convictions of the majority of people. Descartes was not, therefore, single-handedly the reason why people believed what they believed and still believe; but he was the most prominent spokesman, theoretician, inspiration and defender of ideas which people have been able to incorporate into their lives. And because of the theoretical support that he provided, the triumph of those ideas was all the more certain, and all the more complete.

So how did it happen? Why was this little book so successful, and what are the ideas it contains that have since come to take over the world?

The *Meditations* was written in Latin, and first published in 1641. A French translation 6 years later made it more accessible to the wider public. In both versions the writing is simple and clear, with very few technical terms. More importantly, the format and presentation of the *Meditations* make it immediately engaging for the reader: the text doesn't lecture us or inform us, but tells us the story of a quest, and it invites us – requires us, even – to follow the train of thought, and to think through the issues with the narrator. As well as making for a lively read, that fact about its presentation is also of huge political importance: Descartes is telling us that we can and should think for ourselves, that knowledge and understanding are not the preserve of the cloistered academic, but are accessible to the middle-class laymen who were increasingly asserting their political, economic and intellectual independence [3.1.1; 3.1.2].

But for all his radicalism, Descartes is also a very shrewd political operator. By such devices as leaving France, disguising his heliocentrism, presenting the *Meditations* as a religious text with religious objectives, and at the same time inviting criticism from all and sundry (including the religious establishment) in the *Objections and Replies*, he is able to stifle a lot of the criticism he would otherwise have encountered, and so to buy time for the new ideas to take root.

So what, finally, are the ideas that are central to the *Meditations*, which were new or not widely shared when it was written, and which have since achieved the status of beliefs which are so universally accepted that we hardly notice any more that we hold them?

Some of the most obvious are what we might call Descartes' *Metaphysics of Science*. He held, for example, as most of us do but most of his contemporaries didn't, that

- Natural science must be quantitative, not qualitative: we don't explain the way ice feels to the touch by the inherent property of coldness it possesses, but by the (quantifiable) speed with which its particles are moving; we don't explain the colour of grass by its essential greenness, but by the (quantifiable) pressure of light rays which rebound from it.
- The reality of nature cannot be accurately described in ordinary, day-to-day language, but only in the specialized vocabulary of the expert. Thus 'cold' becomes 'with a temperature of x degrees'; 'green' becomes 'reflecting light with such-and-such a wavelength'.
- The behaviour of macroscopic objects depends on that of their microscopic and submicroscopic components.
- The processes we observe in nature are all of them the result of unchanging deterministic laws.
- The basic facts of nature can only be expressed mathematically.

But those ideas were not unique to Descartes. And although they provide the essential background and motivation for the *Meditations*, they are not very obvious when you read it. Here are two other sets of ideas which we now take for granted, and which are not only specifically Cartesian, but are precisely the conclusions he argues for in the text.

The Epistemology of Science

- Descartes thinks human beings can have genuine objective knowledge of the world – we can go beyond how things seem to us, whether as individuals or as groups, and can find out how they really are in themselves.
- Such knowledge is to be obtained not from religion, and not from any other kind of authority – not from tradition or from the accumulated wisdom of the ages – but from the kind of rational analysis of nature that we nowadays call natural science.

Philosophical Anthropology

- Descartes represents each one of us as inhabiting a private world of subjectivity. That private world is the world of feeling, and of the self: what we are for other people is a mere appearance, an outer show; what we really are in ourselves, our true nature, our personality, is something we alone have direct access to, we alone can truly know.
- That private self is what we really are. And yet at the same time much of it we must constantly strive to overcome:
  - If we want to know reality we must use our Reason to escape from the subjective world of feelings and emotions and discover the objective truth;
  - The good life, the moral life, involves putting aside our feelings and our desires, and doing what Reason tells us is the right thing to do.[4]

2. THE MEDITATIONS AND RECENT PHILOSOPHY

An idea that is controversial and new in one age can later achieve the status of something so obvious that no-one any longer bothers to write about it. When that happens the origin of the idea almost always seems to get lost: if something is obvious to everybody, we feel as if it didn't need to be discovered or invented. And if we then go back and read the words of those who originally came up with the idea, we are very likely to misunderstand what they are trying to tell us. That kind of process seems to be what has happened with the reading of Descartes since the eighteenth century.

By the mid-nineteenth century at least, the battles that Descartes devoted his life to fighting had very largely been won. The Enlightenment had happened, and all the points I listed in the last section as Ideas that Made the Modern World had come to be accepted by the great majority of those who thought about such things. More importantly, they were well on the way to being incorporated into political and economic institutions, into social organizations, into education, religion, popular culture and the arts.[5] Against that changed background, the reputation of Descartes also started to change.

In the philosophical establishment, readings of the *Meditations* – like readings of everything else – have differed between the Analytic and Continental traditions. In the Anglophone, Analytic world what came to be called Descartes' 'scientific' writings were generally ignored on the grounds that modern researches had rendered them obsolete, and philosophers who took for granted the idea that scientific knowledge is both possible and important came round to thinking that his Herculean efforts to establish just that conclusion must mean something entirely different. They, therefore, came to represent Descartes as primarily an epistemologist, and to see the *Meditations* as being concerned not with the practical question of whom we should believe, but with the higher, 'philosophical' question of the Foundations of Knowledge. Using a distinction originally deriving from Kant, Descartes was classified as a 'Continental Rationalist' philosopher who claimed that all knowledge is ultimately grounded in the *a priori*, as distinct from the 'British Empiricists' who said it all depends on experience.[6]

In the Continental tradition the importance of the *Meditations* has always tended to be much more on what I have called his Philosophical Anthropology. His creation of the subjective self and his stress on the data of introspection led to his being hailed rather implausibly as the founder of Phenomenology, and therefore of Existentialism and all that has followed it.

More recently the Analytic/Continental divide has shown some signs of closing, and partly as a result of that and partly as a cause, English-speaking philosophers have started to take a much more historically sensitive reading of the classic texts, as a result of which it seems to me that Descartes is coming to be seen as a much more interesting thinker than the caricature that reigned when I was a lad.[7] I hope this book manages to capture some of that interest.

CHAPTER 5

FURTHER READING

1. THE MEDITATIONS

Many different editions and translations are available. The standard (Latin) edition is

- Adam, C. and Tannery, P., eds. *Oeuvres de Descartes* (Paris, Cerf, 1897–1909; new edition Paris, Vrin, 1964–74), vol. VII. (French translation, approved by Descartes, is in vol. IX.)

The standard modern English version is

- Cottingham, J., Stoothoff, R. and Murdoch, D., eds. and trans. *The Philosophical Writings of Descartes* (Cambridge, CUP, 1984), vol. II.

The same translation is also available in the single-volume

- Cottingham, J., Stoothoff, R. and Murdoch, D., eds. and trans. *Descartes: Selected Philosophical Writings* (Cambridge, CUP, 1988).

2. RELATED WORKS BY DESCARTES

[Abbreviations used in the text are given in square brackets.]
There is a version of the story of the Meditations in

- *Discourse on the Method* [*Discourse*], and early parts of
- *Principles of Philosophy* [*Principles*].

The 90-page *Meditations* was published with over 500 pages of

- *Objections and Replies* [OR], which provide a mass of explanations and amplifications. The Objections by various contemporaries range from telling to dull, and Descartes' Replies from sycophantic through helpful to dismissive.

For Descartes' Mechanism, see

- *The World*
- *Treatise on Man*
- *Description of the Human Body*
- *Optics*, and parts 2–4 of
- *Principles of Philosophy*.

For his Epistemology and Metaphysics,

- *Conversation with Burman*
- *The Search for Truth* [*Search*]
- *Comments on a Certain Broadsheet* [*Comments*]
- *Rules for the Direction of our Native Intelligence*

Descartes' Physiology, Psychology and Ethics are covered in

- *The Passions of the Soul* [*Passions*]

In his massive

- *Correspondence*, he writes about just about everything.

3. SOME USEFUL SECONDARY READING

Books on Descartes and the *Meditations*

- Cottingham, J. *Descartes* (Oxford, Blackwell, 1986)
- Curley, E.M. *Descartes against the Skeptics* (Oxford, Blackwell, 1978)
- Dicker, G. *Descartes, an Analytic and Historical Introduction* (New York and Oxford, OUP, 1993)
- Garber, D. *Descartes' Metaphysical Physics* (Chicago, UCP, 1992)
- Gaukroger, S. *Descartes: An Intellectual Biography* (Oxford, OUP, 1995)
- Hatfield, G. *Descartes and the* Meditations (London, Routledge, 2003)
- Williams, B. *Descartes: The Project of Pure Enquiry* (Harmondsworth, Penguin, 1978)
- Wilson, C. *Descartes'* Meditations: *An Introduction* (Cambridge, CUP, 2003)
- Wilson, M.D. *Descartes* (London, Routledge, 1978)

Collections of Articles

- Chappell, V. ed. *Descartes' Meditations: Critical Essays* (Lanham, New York, Boulder and Oxford, Rowman & Littlefield, 1997)
- Cottingham, J. ed. *The Cambridge Companion to Descartes* (Cambridge, CUP, 1992)
- Doney, W. ed. *Descartes: A Collection of Critical Essays* (London and Basingstoke, Macmillan, 1967)
- Hooker, M. ed. *Descartes: Critical and Interpretive Essays* (Baltimore and London, Johns Hopkins UP, 1978)
- Rorty, A.O. ed. *Essays on Descartes' Meditations* (Berkeley, UCP, 1986)
- Sorell, T. ed. *Descartes* (Aldershot, Ashgate, 1999)
- Voss, S. ed. *Essays on the Philosophy and Science of René Descartes* (New York and Oxford, OUP, 1993)

4. OTHER WORKS REFERRED TO IN THE TEXT

- Aquinas, T. *Summa Theologiae*
- Ayer, A.J. *Language, Truth and Logic*
- Berkeley, G. *A Treatise Concerning the Principles of Human Knowledge*
- Bouwsma, O.K. "Descartes' Evil Genius", in *Philosophical Review* 1949
- Eddington, A.S. *The Nature of the Physical World* (Cambridge, CUP, 1929)
- Fèbvre, L. *Le Problème de l'incroyance au XVIe siècle*
- Galileo, G. *Il Saggiatore* (The Assayer), in Drake, S. and O'Malley, C.D. eds. and trans. *The Controversy on the Comets of 1618* (Philadelphia, U Pennsylvania Press, 1960)
- Hume, D. *A Treatise of Human Nature*
- Kant, I. *Critique of Pure Reason*
- Kuhn, T.S. *The Structure of Scientific Revolutions*
- Lichtenberg, G.C. Aphorisms, in Grenzmann, W. ed. *Gesammelte Werke* (Frankfurt am Main, Holle Verlag, 1949)
- Locke, J. *An Essay Concerning Human Understanding*
- Malebranche, N. 6th Éclaircissement, in Rodis-Lewis, G. ed. *Oeuvres Complètes* (Paris, Vrin, 1964), vol. 3.

- Mersenne, M. *L'Impiété des Déistes, Athées et Libertins de ce Temps* (Stuttgart-Bad Cannstatt, Frommann/Holzboog, 1975)
- Popper, K. *Conjectures and Refutations*
- Putnam, H. *Reason, Truth and History*
- Ryle, G. *Dilemmas* (Cambridge, CUP, 1954)
- Sellars, W. *Science, Perception and Reality*
- Wittgenstein, L. *Philosophical Investigations*

NOTES

1: THE *MEDITATIONS* IN CONTEXT

[1] '. . . [I]f the view is false, so too are the entire foundations of my philosophy' (To Mersenne, 11/1633;I.271).

2: OVERVIEW OF THEMES

[1] The crucial text for this idea is Kuhn.

[2] My own view is that the belief in the possibility of an 'objective' view is a myth. Instead of guaranteeing the possibility of agreement between people, it has become a device for excluding from consideration the views of those who disagree with us most radically, and so have most to teach us.

3: READING THE TEXT

[1] The *Discourse*, where a very similar story is told, begins 'I am presenting this work only as a history [*histoire*] or, if you prefer, a fable . . .' (1;VI.4).

[2] Johannes Kepler (1571–1630). Best known for his laws of planetary motion, published between 1609 and 1619.

[3] Galileo Galilei (1564–1642). Most famous for telescopic observations supporting heliocentrism.

[4] Read the *Dedicatory Letter*, and ask how sincere it is – especially the remark about unbelievers and circularity (2).

[5] Descartes proposes a kind of philosophical Reformation: God's work in Nature is available to everyone just by consulting his/her own intelligence, without the need for mediation through the Church.

[6] 'This doubt should not be applied to ordinary life. [It] should be kept in check, and employed solely in connection with the contemplation of the truth' (*Principles*, 1.3).

[7] Descartes distinguishes 'the sciences' (*les sciences*), where we 'make reliable judgements on the basis of knowledge we already possess', from other areas of knowledge where we merely accumulate information (*Search*, X.503). The three principal branches of 'the sciences' are 'medicine, mechanics and morals' (*Principles*, Pref.; IXb.14).

[8] Elsewhere the Argument from Error and the Dream Argument seem much more on a par {*Discourse*, 4; *Principles*, 1.4.}.

[9] 'There seem to be no marks by means of which we can with certainty distinguish being asleep from being awake' (*Principles*, 1.4).

[10] Descartes does use the expression, not in quite the modern sense {*Le Monde*, 7;XI.47}.

¹¹ Elsewhere {*Principles*, 1.5} the two moves are separated, and the structure of the argument is clearer.

¹² Notice that the Demon does not appear in *Discourse* or *Principles*.

¹³ This is not to say you can't doubt your own sanity. (I often do.) But that involves thinking, coherently, that your mental processes are unreliable. That is very different from the unthinkable thought that none of your thoughts has any meaning – including that one.

¹⁴ Much of the division between 'Analytic' and 'Continental' philosophy arises from just this question.

¹⁵ The relation of this kind of doubt to Descartes is tenuous. It isn't the position at the end of Meditation 1, which he summarizes with the image of the Malicious Demon, because that doesn't take our *a priori* knowledge as given [3.1.6]. And it isn't the position of Meditation 6, before he proves the existence of the material world, because by that stage he has re-established a secure system of knowledge based on empirical science [3.5.1]. It corresponds roughly to the position immediately after the Dream Argument, before he knocks away *a priori* knowledge with the Nature Argument [3.1.3; 3.1.5].

¹⁶ The currency analogy is taken from Ryle, 7 (p. 94).

¹⁷ The story is from Bouwsma.

¹⁸ Some have taken this to be Descartes' own position – the only things we really know are Absolute Certainties and what can be infallibly deduced from them. That would mean that scientific knowledge – the very kind of knowledge that he is trying to validate in his writings, and which he thinks is *not* Absolutely Certain (*Principles*, 4.204–6) – is impossible and not worth trying to attain, and also that we have no knowledge of particular contingent facts, which he claims we do [3.4.5; 3.6.4].

¹⁹ This argument is often read into the *Meditations*, but doesn't actually appear there. The rationale behind The Thinker's quest is psychological ('To remove doubt and uncertainty, you need to find something you can't question'), not logical ('No belief is justified unless some beliefs need no justification').

²⁰ '. . . [T]his grand book – I mean the universe – . . . is written in the language of mathematics' (Galileo, 183–4).

²¹ It occurs in *Principles*, 1.7, and (in French) in *Discourse*, 4 (VI. 32).

²² The original has *'necessario esse verum'*/*'est nécessairement vraie'* and *'necessario sum'*/*'moi qui suis certain que je suis'* (25; IXa.18–19).

²³ And a deeper question: in striving for an objective view, do we mean one with no presuppositions? Or only one with *appropriate* presuppositions, openly acknowledged? Which do we mean when we say that objectivity is important in a referee, a judge, a doctor or an historian?

²⁴ His earlier fame was more in line with his ambitions. His reputation as 'The Father of Modern Philosophy' was gained at a time when it meant something more like the father of modern *science*.

²⁵ Parts of it survive, and have been published. They give a clear, readable, view of the system. See *The World* and *Treatise on Man*.

[72] Many have tried to locate the facts of experience not in what is observed, but in our observings of it: I can doubt whether the litmus paper is red, but not that I'm having a red experience. (C.f. Descartes' remark that he can doubt the lamp, but not that he is having an experience as of seeing a lamp (28–9) [3.2.3].) Can such moments of private certainty – if they exist – provide objective empirical data?

[73] Descartes goes on to say that because his conclusions can all be demonstrated as following from the simplest principles of human knowledge, they are *more* than practically certain, on a par with mathematical proofs (*Principles*, 4. 206).

[74] Again we see how Platonic Descartes' view of things is: real knowledge is not of actual things in the actual world, but of timeless realities which lie behind them. Is that the way you see the job of science? Notice how he again echoes the Platonic idea of knowledge by *recollection*: 'the truth of these matters is so open and so much in harmony with my nature, that on first discovering them it seems that I am not so much learning something new as remembering what I knew before' (64).

[75] In *Principles*, 1.4–18 the two arguments are presented in reverse order. OR1; 101 calls the Meditation 3 proof his 'chief' (*praecipuam/ principale*) argument.

[76] It appears in St Anselm of Canterbury's *Proslogion* of 1077–8 (§1–5), and has been talked about on and off ever since.

[77] Many philosophers think that if 'God' is the name of an individual being, then it doesn't *have* a meaning: names have no content, they just refer to their bearers, in the same way as pointing at them does. I think the Ontological Argument can still be made out if you take that view, but it would take longer and be less clear.

[78] Nicolas de Malebranche (1638–1715) was an avowed Cartesian who thought Descartes' 'proof' of matter showed only that its existence is very probable (*tout-à-fait vrai-semblable* – 63–4). George Berkeley (1685–1753) argued that matter does not, and *could* not exist (e.g. 4–24). Berkeley's 'Idealism', though, has almost nothing in common with later versions such as those of Kant and Hegel – which shows what a potentially misleading term it is.

[79] See early-twentieth-century 'Logical Positivists', such as Ayer.

[80] Berkeley always claimed that his Idealism saved us from the Scepticism into which we must otherwise necessarily fall.

[81] A natural one is to question what it means for God to be 'perfect'. In fact, given the seventeenth-century understanding of the terms we translate that way, this is actually one of the *strongest* points of Descartes' argument. The word derives from a Latin root meaning 'made', 'finished', 'completed' or 'actualized', so to say that God is perfect virtually *means* that God is real. (The expression 'reality or perfection', appears several times in the French version of the *Meditations* – for example, IXa.32 – and in other works.)

[82] See A592–602; B620–31.

83 This is why, in modern systems of formal logic, existence is expressed not as a predicate but by use of quantifiers.

84 This separation of Understanding and Imagination, and the downgrading of the latter as misleading, carnal, the work of the material body as opposed to the pure, God-like understanding which seeks the truth, is of course typical of the Enlightenment's downgrading of the sensitive, emotional, imaginative aspects of human beings, with consequences for the ways we think about things like art, creativity, and men and women.

85 'Strictly speaking, a *real* distinction exists only between two or more substances' *Principles* 1.60.

86 Is that a genuine distinction? Are there facts of logic which are something more than just facts about the judgements people make (and specifically about the judgements that *certain kinds* of people make)?

87 See footnote 78 [3.5.4].

88 Hobbes said God *could* deceive us in such a matter, just as doctors sometimes deceive their patients for the patients' own good (OR3; 195).

89 Berkeley thought that far from being natural, the belief in matter – something which is not itself directly experienced but which underlies the experiences we do have – was in fact a relatively recent mistake resulting from bad philosophical theories (like that of Descartes) [3.5.4].

90 Like God before him, Descartes labours for 6 days, and rests on the seventh.

91 Eddington, xi–xiii.

92 Sellars, 1.2.

4: RECEPTION AND INFLUENCE OF THE *MEDITATIONS*

1 What upset the authorities most seems to have been his demystifying of transubstantiation.

2 Opinions differ as to how useful the Cartesian model was. In the Biological sciences Descartes' mechanism is generally seen as a research programme that failed, providing too crude and clumsy a model for the explanation of living systems. In the Physical sciences, too, something similar applies: his heroic attempt to banish all mysterious forces, powers and sympathies from nature, and to replace them with a system based on nothing but matter in motion, collapsed in the face of Newton's synthesis, centred around the inexplicable, 'occult' notion of 'Gravity'.

3 Others (most obviously that of Aristotle) have lasted longer, but we have also to take into account the number of people whose lives these ideas have informed.

4 This is in fact less true of Descartes' own moral works than it is of the way the kind of Dualism he described has been developed.

⁵ Think about the way the points I listed above feed into things as diverse as the university curriculum, the pronouncements of moralists, the form of the novel, or the funding of science.

⁶ A large part of this story involves the changing meanings of the term 'Reason'. For Descartes it meant the rational analysis of experience that we later came to call 'science', but later, especially after Kant, it came to be reserved for pure *a priori* reasoning.

⁷ Interestingly, Descartes has tended to be most accurately represented outside of mainstream philosophy. Non-professional philosophers, historians and literary theorists have, I think, correctly seen him as the great defender of Reason: the man whose ideas have the effect of downplaying art and morality to mere feeling, and of representing animals as mere robots that we can exploit at our convenience.

INDEX

a priori knowledge
  dubitability of 23–4, 48, 89,
    94–5
  and knowledge of nature 140,
    143, 148–9, 152, 161
  nature and status of 20–3, 26,
    47, 92–4
  see also doubt, 'hyperbolical'
'accident' 100n46
'Analytic' vs. 'Continental'
  Philosophy 33n14, 177–8
Anselm of Canterbury, St. 150–1,
  157–8
anthropomorphism 125–8, 130
Aquinas, St. Thomas 127n61
Aristotelian science 41–4
  Descartes' opposition to 2–4,
    10–11, 58, 141
Aristotle 98n45, 131n63, 174n3
  on the 'soul' 68–9
  see also Aristotelian science
Arnauld, Antoine 135
atheism 59, 122, 128
  Descartes as atheist 120–1
  and knowledge 124, 152
  modern-day 115–17
  possibility of 123–4, 126–8
  and rationality 117–9
  seventeenth-century 114–15
  see also God
Ayer, Sir Alfred J 155n79

Berkeley, George 86, 153–6,
  165n89, 174
Bouwsma, O.K. 37n17
Brahe, Tycho 1
Bruno, Giordano 114

causal adequacy principle 98–9,
  100–1, 105–6
certainty
  and Clear and Distinct Ideas
    89–92
  and *Cogito* 45–50, 57, 89–90
  kinds of 15–17, 38–9
  and scepticism 17, 28, 30–1,
    39–41, 137–9, 152
  and science 141, 142–5, 146–9
  of sense vs. reason 18–23, 23–4,
    26–7, 58, 93
  see also doubt, 'hyperbolical';
    dream argument; nature
    argument
Christina, Queen of Sweden 2
circle, Cartesian 135–7
Clear and Distinct Ideas 83,
  96n40, 111, 129, 148, 151,
  162–3, 165
  nature of 89–92
  role of 92–4, 132–4, 142–5,
    165–8
  see also circle, Cartesian;
    doubt, 'hyperbolical'
cogito, ergo sum 45–50, 51–2,
  74–7, 81–4, 89–94, 151
*Comments on a Certain
  Broadsheet* 180
conception vs.
  comprehension 107,
  109–10
consciousness 46, 50–2, 57, 71–2,
  79–81, 109, 160–3
conservation 60, 101, 108, 110–11,
  122–4
Conversation with Burman 180

'Continental' Philosophy *see*
'Analytic' vs. 'Continental'
Philosophy
Correspondence 180
creation *see* conservation
criterion, problem of the 90–1

demon, malicious 24–6,
29–30, 34–8, 45, 48, 51,
75, 154
Descartes, René
influence of 172–8
life 1–4
relation of philosophy to
science 3
*Description of the Human
Body* 70n28, 180
Discourse on Method 10n1,
25n12, 46n21, 58, 174, 179
doubt
'hyperbolical' 94–5, 129–30,
135–9, 170
method of 11–17, 24, 54
see also scepticism, disproof of
Dream Argument 18–21, 24, 25,
31–4, 34–8, 82, 92, 148–9,
151, 153, 166–8
dualism 67–74, 177n4
see also mind

Earth, motion of 1, 3, 7, 14–15,
43, 93, 115
Eddington, Sir Arthur 169
Einstein, Albert 66
elements 60n26
emanation 124, 127
eminent 102n50
empiricism 178
Enlightenment 7, 162n84, 177
error
argument from 19, 151
nature and avoidance of 130–4
evil, problem of 132n65

experience, content vs. context
of 32–4
see also sensory knowledge

Fèbvre, Lucien 114n56

Galileo 1, 2–3, 10, 43n20, 94, 115
condemnation of 10, 58, 120
Gassendi, Pierre 143n70
Gaukroger, Stephen 115
God 10, 15, 72, 83, 98, 103–4,
131–2, 155, 163–5
attributes of 125–8
Descartes' first proof of 102,
104–9, 111
meaning of belief in 115–17,
120–5, 126
nature of existence of 111–14
and objectivity 8, 66–7, 89, 95,
129–30, 135–40, 171
'ontological' argument
for 149–51, 152, 156–8
rationality of belief in 117–19
see also atheism; conception vs.
comprehension;
conservation; religion

Halley, Edmund 141–2
Harvey, William 1
Hegel, Georg Wilhelm
Friedrich 153n78
Hobbes, Thomas 79n,
165n88
Hume, David 139n67, 174
'hypothetico-deductive
method' 141–5

idealism 148–9, 151, 152–6, 164
ideas, kinds of 96–8
imagination 97, 159, 160–2
immaterial existents 71, 78–80,
88
infinity 106–7, 109–10

'innate' knowledge 22, 91, 93,
96n, 97–8, 106–7, 108–9,
126, 162
interaction, of mind and body 73

justification
problem of 136–7
regress of 40

Kant, Immanuel 118, 153n78,
156–8, 174, 178
Kepler, Johannes 1, 3, 10, 94
knowledge, foundations of 14
Kuhn, Thomas 7n1

language 72
and ontology 77
laws of nature 3, 14, 59–60, 111,
116, 120–4, 134, 147, 149,
164, 176
Leibniz, Gottfried Willhelm
von 67, 174
Lichtenberg, Georg 75
Locke, John 98, 106, 174
logical form 156–8
logical positivism 155n

madness, and doubt 29–30
Malebranche, Nicolas de 153,
164, 174
Manichaeism 128n
mathematics
Descartes as mathematician 2,
173
mathematisation of nature 41,
55, 60, 65, 146–7, 160–1, 176
Matrix, The 34–8
matter
existence of 18–20, 84, 96n40,
103–4, 118–19, 147–9,
152–6, 159, 163–5
nature of 53, 55, 58–62, 68,
147, 160–1

mechanism 41, 55, 58–62, 65, 70,
102n49, 121, 173
Meditations on First Philosophy
aims of 7–8, 10, 55, 58–9, 140,
146–7, 178
'Big Question' of 8, 15, 168–71
dialogue form in 18–19
as fiction 9–11
influence of 172–8
Mersenne, Marin 114
mind
nature of, for Descartes 50–3,
67–74, 160–2
other minds 82n32, 102–4
separation from body 52–3,
57, 77–84, 162–3
significance of Descartes'
theory of 8, 43, 57, 66–7,
104, 170–1, 177–8
miracles 121
mistakes see error
modes 86–7, 97, 100
monism 67–8, 88
morality 15n7, 66, 72, 74,
115, 124, 127–8, 132, 145,
177n4

nature argument 23–4, 136, 151
see also doubt, 'hyperbolical'
necessary truths 47–8, 76, 83–4,
156
Newton, Sir Isaac 2, 173

objectivity 4, 34–8, 43, 54n23,
95, 135–9, 168–71
problem of 5–8
see also relativism
Objections & Replies 175
omnipotence 121, 126–7,
132n65
omniscience 127, 132n65
ontology 67–8, 76–7, 84–8,
99–100, 111–14

perfection 98, 106–7, 108, 125–8, 149–50, 157
and reality 156n81
pineal gland 73n29
Plato, Platonism 90n35, 91n36, 149n74, 151, 164
and the 'scientific revolution' 3, 170
pluralism 67–8, 87
Popper, Karl 142n69
primary & secondary qualities 62–7, 102n, 147, 149, 160–1
Principles of Philosophy 10, 174
psychology vs. logic 15–16, 40n19, 50, 82, 90–2, 163
Putnam, Hilary 101n48

rationalism 143, 178
real distinction 68, 162–3
realism
vs. anti-realism 37
indirect 56
'reality' (= substantiality) 99–100
'reformation', philosophical 13n5
Regius (Henri le Roi) 98n42
relativism 6–8, 30–1, 38–41, 137–40
see also objectivity
religion and science 41, 43, 121–4, 132
Ryle, Gilbert 35n16

scepticism 4, 14, 17, 26, 27–31, 115
'Cartesian' 31, 34–8, 148, 156
defined 27–8
disproof of 129–30, 137–9, 151–2
global 29–30
history of 28
'scholastics' 42, 99

science
Cartesian vs. scholastic 41–3, 58–9, 131n
Descartes' theory of 140–5, 148–9, 176
Descartes' work in 2–4, 140, 173–7
and objectivity 6–7, 134
see also religion
'scientific revolution' 3, 43, 170
Search for Truth 180
sections, of *Meditations* vii
self 50–3, 98, 102–4, 177
existence of 74–7, 79–80
see also cogito ergo sum; mind
Sellars, Wilfrid 169–70
sensory knowledge
certainty of 18–23, 31–4, 93–4, 165–8
nature of 53–4, 55–7, 159–62
and science 41–4
Sextus Empiricus 28
soul 68–9
see also mind
space and matter 59–62
Spinoza, Baruch 67, 86, 115, 174
substance 67–8, 81, 86–8, 98–100, 123, 162–3

Thinker, The 9–11
transubstantiation 123n60, 173n1
Treatise on Man 58n25, 180

vacuum, impossibility of 61–2
vat, brain in a 31, 34

will
and error 72–3, 130–4
freedom of 73, 132n
Wittgenstein, Ludwig 95n37
World, The 58, 59, 63, 180